Charles Prestwood Lucas

Introduction to a Historical Geography of the British Colonies

Charles Prestwood Lucas

Introduction to a Historical Geography of the British Colonies

ISBN/EAN: 9783742811875

Manufactured in Europe, USA, Canada, Australia, Japa

Cover: Foto ©ninafisch / pixelio.de

Manufactured and distributed by brebook publishing software (www.brebook.com)

Charles Prestwood Lucas

Introduction to a Historical Geography of the British Colonies

Clarendon Press Series

INTRODUCTION

TO A

HISTORICAL GEOGRAPHY

OF THE

BRITISH COLONIES

BY

C. P. LUCAS, B.A.

OF BALLIOL COLLEGE, OXFORD
AND THE COLONIAL OFFICE, LONDON

Oxford

AT THE CLARENDON PRESS

1887

[*All rights reserved*]

PREFACE.

THIS little book is intended as the first instalment of a Historical Geography of the British Colonies. Any succeeding parts will be more purely geographical and will deal with the separate divisions of the Empire.

I know no book which gives quite simply and shortly a connected account of the Colonies, of the geographical and historical reasons of their belonging to England, and of the special place which each colony holds in the Empire. The present is an attempt to supply the want from materials to hand at the Colonial Office and elsewhere.

C. P. LUCAS.

May, 1887.

Note to p. 39, l. 31.—Since this paragraph was written, slavery in Cuba has been abolished by law.

BOOKS RELATING TO COLONIAL SUBJECTS.

THE subjoined list of some well-known books relating to colonial subjects may be useful to teachers and students:—

The annual *Colonial Office List*, published by Messrs. Harrison & Sons, contains much general and useful information, together with maps of most of the colonies: the issue for 1887 has been considerably revised and enlarged.

The various Handbooks published in connexion with the Colonial and Indian Exhibition, and the volume compiled under the authority of the Royal Commission, and entitled *Her Majesty's Colonies*, are familiar to the public.

Among older standard books are:—

HEEREN's *Political System of Europe and its Colonies*, which groups together clearly the events of different periods and the work of different nations, giving the authorities in each case.

The same writer's *Researches of Asiatic nations* and *African nations* give full accounts of Phœnician and Carthaginian colonisation.

MERIVALE's Lectures on *Colonisation and Colonies* are well known.

SIR G. C. LEWIS's *Essay on the Government of Dependencies* is full of history and political philosophy: it ought to be specially valuable in connexion with the teaching for the Final Classical Schools at Oxford.

The chapter in ADAM SMITH's *Wealth of Nations* entitled *Of Colonies*, and especially the second part, *On the Causes of the Prosperity of New Colonies*, will of course be consulted.

viii BOOKS RELATING TO COLONIAL SUBJECTS.

RAYNAL's History of *The Settlements and Trade of the Europeans in the East and West Indies* yields a great deal of information mixed with much of little value.

HELPS' *Spanish Conquest of America* contains an account of early Portuguese exploration on the West Coast of Africa, as well as the history of the Spaniards in America, and a full record of the treatment of the native races, etc.

Among later publications :—

SIR G. BIRDWOOD's Report on the *Miscellaneous old Records of the India Office, Nov.* 1, 1878, printed by the Government, contains a most complete and interesting summary of early European colonisation in the East.

DOYLE's *History of the English in America*, 1882, gives in the earlier chapters accounts of the first European voyages to and settlements in North America.

La Colonisation scientifique et les Colonies françaises, by BORDIER, dated Paris 1884, gives suggestive information as to climate, race, and other factors in colonisation.

It is needless to mention PROFESSOR SEELEY's *Expansion of England.*

Among smaller publications :—

Colonies and Dependencies (in the 'English Citizen' series), by J. S. COTTON and E. J. PAYNE ; RANSOME's Lectures on *Our Colonies and India*; and SIR RAWSON RAWSON's *Inaugural Address to the Statistical Society, on British and Foreign Colonies,* delivered in November 1884, and published by Messrs. Stanford, ought to be noticed. The last especially gives a vast amount of information in small space, and is accompanied by several useful diagrams.

Lastly, it is perhaps allowable to remind those interested in the subject of the various books of the invaluable Hakluyt series, and of the separate articles of the *Encyclopædia Britannica.*

TABLE OF CONTENTS.

CHAPTER I.
                                                              PAGE

What is a Colony 1

    SEC. 1. Colony and Plantation.—2. Definition of colony.—3. How far are the British colonies colonies in the true sense? 4. Popular use of the term colony.

CHAPTER II.

Motives of Colonisation 4

    SECS. 1-2. Four main motives of colonisation.—3. First motive—love of adventure—as a rule the earliest in point of time: it influences individuals more than governments or companies.—4-8. Second motive—desire of wealth: commerce has led (1) to system and permanence, (2) to formation of companies, and (3) to government taking part in colonisation.—9. Third motive—political and social discontent.—10-13. Fourth motive—religion—has led (1) to exploration, (2) to conquest, and (3) to settlement: in some cases it has been a barrier between the mother country and the colony, in others it has been a link between them.

CHAPTER III.

Climate and Race 15

    SEC. 1. Different climates suit different races.—2. Different climates lead to different dependencies of the same people.—3. A race, to colonise, must have (1) strong physique and power of expansion, (2) certain special qualities—4. Six special characteristics of colonising races:—5-8. (1) Enterprise—mixed breeds are enterprising, as also maritime peoples, and small states; the most successful colonisers have been the least state-ridden: 9. (2) Aptitude for trade: 10. (3) Readiness to emigrate: 11. (4) Capacity for fighting: 12. (5) Power of assimilation: 13. (6) Capacity for ruling.

CHAPTER IV.

Modes of colonising and kinds of colonists . . . 28

SEC. 1. Three modes of colonising:—(a) by individuals—they have generally been protected by the state;—2. (b) by the state; —3. And (c) by chartered companies.—4. Classes of inhabitants in a colony:—natives, causes which lead to their good or bad treatment—5. Three classes of immigrants:—6-8. First class— free settlers; they may be classified on the basis of Heeren's division of colonies—Agriculturists, Planters, Sheep and cattle farmers, Miners, Traders:—9. Second class—Slaves:—10-11 Third class—(a) Convicts—(b) Indentured coolies.

CHAPTER V.

Nations which have colonised.—1. Ancient . . . 47

SEC. 1. Nations which have colonised.—2. Ancient colonisation: —the Mediterranean peoples; 3. The Phœnicians; 4. The Carthaginians—two classes of Carthaginian colonies,—comparison of Carthaginians with Venetians and Dutch; 5. The Greeks—two classes of Greek colonies, (1) the ἀποικίαι or colonies proper, (2) the Athenian κληρουχίαι; 6. The Romans. —the Roman coloniæ—four stages of coloniæ, (1) the *coloniæ civium Romanorum*, (2) the Latin colonies, (3) the Gracchan colonies, (4) the later Roman colonies.

CHAPTER VI.

Nations which have colonised.—2. Modern . . . 60

SEC. 1. Beginnings of modern colonisation.—2. The Spaniards and Portuguese.—3-7. Spanish colonisation—extent and nature of Spanish colonial empire—defects of Spanish colonisation—good points in the colonial policy of Spain—general results.—8-13. Portuguese colonisation—Prince Henry the Navigator—expansion of Portugal—extent and nature of Portuguese colonial empire—the East—Brazil—the Portuguese compared with the Spaniards—their merits as colonisers—

their defects—special causes of their decline—general results.—
14-19. Dutch colonisation—Dutch contrasted with Spaniards
and Portuguese—extent and nature of the Dutch colonial empire
—the East—the West—trading instincts of the Dutch—Dutch
East India Company—causes of Dutch successes—causes of
their decline—general results.—20-28. French colonisation—
French compared with Spaniards and Dutch—rivalry between
France and England—extent and nature of French colonial
empire—the French government and the French nation—
aptitude of French people for colonising—causes which led to
failure of French colonisation—faults of the government—want
of definite policy—religious exclusiveness—want of harmony
between the government and the nation—French colonies at the
present day.

CHAPTER VII.

English Colonisation 91

SEC. 1. English colonisation—its success due to the country and the
race.—2. Main features of Great Britain and its inhabitants.—
3. Early English explorers.—4. Lateness of English colonisation compared with that of other races.—5-6. Three periods
of English colonisation—first period the 17th century: results
of that period—Newfoundland—Nova Scotia—West Indies
and Bermudas—West Coast of Africa—St. Helena—India:
first colonisation of the United States—special characteristics
of English colonisation in the 17th century.—7-10. Second
period of English colonisation, 1700-1814—its main characteristics—the struggle between France and England—loss of
United States: first half of the period to 1763—its results—
Gibraltar—West Indies—Canada—India? second half of the
period 1763-1814—its results—Malta—St. Lucia—Mauritius
—Ceylon—British Guiana—the Cape—Trinidad—Heligoland
—India—Penang—British Honduras—Sierra Leone: first
colonisation of Australia.—10-16. Third period of English
colonisation, from 1814—its main characteristics; results of
the third period—Ascension—Singapore—Malacca—the Falk-
lands—Aden and Perim—Hongkong—Labuan—Lagos—Fiji
—Cyprus — Canadian Dominion — Australia—New Zealand
—South Africa—Natal—India—Sarawak — British North
Borneo—New Guinea.—17. General results of English
colonisation :—in Europe ; 18. in Asia ; 19. in Africa ; 20.
in America ; 21. in Australasia.—22. General summary.—23.
England has gained by her losses.

CHAPTER VIII.

Changes in the English Colonies during the 19th century . PAGE 119

SEC. 1. Special character of 19th century.—2. Scientific inventions. —3-5. Effect of scientific inventions on the English colonial empire—Ship canals—the Suez Canal—the Panama Canal—the Canadian canals—steam and telegraphic communication—effects of the introduction of steam and electricity upon the mutual relations of the mother country and the colonies.—6-7. Social changes—(1) the abolition of slavery, (2) the anti-transportation movement.—8-13. Political changes—three classes of English colonies—grant of responsible government to the great colonies, connected with free trade policy at home and with the removal of Imperial troops from the colonies—confederation, the great political work of the century—two forms of confederation in regard to the English empire—(1) colonial confederation — requisites for its success: British North America—Australia—South Africa: (2) Imperial confederation.

LIST OF MAPS.

To Face

1. *Map showing the* principal areas of slavery and the principal convict settlements past and present . . . . p. 37
2. —— Greek, Phoenician, and Carthaginian colonies, and the Roman Empire . . . . p. 47
3. —— Spanish and Portuguese colonies past and present . p. 60
4. —— Dutch colonies past and present . . . . p. 74
5. —— French colonies past and present . . . . p. 81
6. —— English colonies at the end of the 17th century . . p. 95
7. —— English colonies in 1814 . . . . . . p. 99
8. —— English colonies at the present day . . . . p. 104

CHAPTER I.

WHAT IS A COLONY?

1. THE English colonies should more correctly be called the English[1] dependencies. All the foreign and colonial possessions of Great Britain are in a sense dependencies, but to most of them the term colony does not strictly apply.

Colony and plantation.

The Latin word 'colonia' implied cultivation of the ground: it is more correctly translated by 'plantation' than by 'colony[2].' The earliest British colonies, those founded in America, were known as plantations; and before the creation of a Secretaryship of State for War and the Colonies at the end of the last century[3], the superintendence of colonial matters was entrusted to a Board or Committee for 'Trade and the Plantations.'

Similarly Bacon entitled his essay on colonisation ' Of Plantations,' ' de plantationibus populorum et coloniis,' though he makes use of the word with reference rather to the planting of men and women than to the planting of the soil. 'Plantation' however has long been superseded by 'colony,' and 'colony' has long ceased to imply, if it ever implied, any purely agricultural meaning.

---

[1] In this book, however, 'dependency' is generally used as the opposite of 'settlement.'

[2] The terms colony and plantation are fully explained by Sir G. Cornewall Lewis, 'Government of Dependencies,' chaps. ii. and iii. in edition of 1841, pp. 114, 115 and 170 etc.

[3] The exact changes which occurred in the arrangements for the management of colonial business will be found in the 'Government of Dependencies,' chap. ii. p. 161, and on p. 9 of the last edition (1887) of the Colonial Office List.

CHAPTER I.

Definition of Colony.

2. In his 'Government of Dependencies[1],' Sir G. Lewis lays down that 'a colony properly denotes a body of persons belonging to one country and political community, who, having abandoned that country and community, form a new and separate society, independent or dependent, in some district which is wholly or nearly uninhabited, or from which they expel the ancient inhabitants.'

Taking this definition, it would seem that a colony in its proper sense implies, firstly, voluntary abandonment of one country; secondly, permanent settlement in another; and thirdly, settlement in a country in which the settlers either from the first form the bulk of the inhabitants, or at least in course of time largely outnumber the natives. It is also clear that the word does not necessarily imply dependence on the mother-country.

How far are the British Colonies colonies in the true sense?

3. Consequently the Eastern colonies of Great Britain are not colonies in the true sense, for the English residents in them have not abandoned their own country, nor have they permanently settled in the East; while the countries in which they have taken up their temporary abode contain a large native population. The same test excludes other parts of the empire, such as the Mediterranean stations and the settlements on the West coast of Africa. Canada, again, is strictly speaking not a colony; for, as far at least as the older province of Quebec is concerned, it belongs to England not in virtue of settlement but by right of conquest. The Australasian colonies have a better title to the name; but it must be remembered even in their case, that some of the earliest settlers in Australia were not voluntary English emigrants but convicts sent out against their will: while the wars with the Maoris, and the fact that they still remain a not unimportant element in the population of New Zealand, might create a doubt as to whether those islands should be classed as settled or as conquered countries.

[1] Chap. iii.

On the other hand, the United States may well be said to be still colonies of Great Britain, colonies which, though they have been planted not in[1] a 'pure soil,' but in one from which the ancient inhabitants have been expelled, are yet permanent voluntary settlements of English origin in a land, the greater part of which now knows no inhabitants but themselves.

4. An account then of the English colonies should properly include the United States, and exclude India and many other divisions of the empire: and though the word colony must in this book be used in its popular sense, as simply equivalent to any foreign possession, it is well to bear in mind the true meaning of the term, for it gives at once a clue to the real character of the various possessions, which compose what has been called Greater Britain.

CHAPTER I.

Popular use of the term colony.

---

[1] See Bacon's Essay on Plantations.

CHAPTER II.

MOTIVES OF COLONISATION.

Four main motives of colonisation.

1. THE main motives of colonisation, which alike in ancient and modern times have led to discovery, to conquest, and to settlement, are four in number; love of enterprise, desire of wealth, social or political discontent, and religion.

2. Of these four, one or other has had greater influence at given periods of history or in certain countries; but hardly even in the minds of the leaders and pioneers of colonisation, much less in those of their followers, has a single motive ever predominated to the exclusion of all the others.

The Greeks, for instance, planted their colonies for commercial purposes as well as to relieve the pressure of population at home. Columbus was not merely an adventurer but also a religious enthusiast. And the motives which led the Puritans to New England were in part social and political as well as religious.

Still it is useful to bear in mind that the river of colonisation has not flowed from one source only; and that from time to time first one tributary and then another has risen in tide and volume, and has given a special colour to the main stream.

First motive, love of adventure.

3. To take these four motives in succession: it is hardly necessary to point out that enterprise, energy, and love of adventure are to be found in certain races, climates, and localities, rather than in others. History has abundantly shown that the white man, for instance, is more enterprising than the black or yellow, that maritime peoples take more

kindly to distant adventure than do dwellers inland, and that CHAPTER
it is the temperate zone, not the tropics or the Arctic regions, II.
which gives birth to the moving spirits of the world.

It is also obvious that discovery must precede conquest or *As a rule
the earliest* settlement: love of enterprise, therefore, would seem to *in point of* come first of the four motives in order of time: although in *time.* view of the fact that the Phoenicians and Greeks and Northmen were from the first merchants rather than explorers, it is impossible to lay down broadly that love of adventure is the prime source of colonisation.

It is natural to suppose, and history has proved, that this motive is strongest in a new age and in a growing country, when some fresh impulse has been given to the minds of men, bidding them look restlessly to the future, to an unknown land and to an age which they hope will be richer and fuller than the present. Spain had been newly consolidated, and was in the full vigour of youth, when her government sent out Columbus to find America. And in England the period of the Reformation and the Revival of learning gave birth to a race of explorers and adventurers, of the type of Drake and Raleigh, whose chivalry and daring made the Elizabethan age the most romantic and picturesque period of English history.

It is further a motive which clearly works on individual men *It in-* rather than on governments or associations of men. Subsidies *fluences in-dividuals* to science may sometimes be given by kings or voted by *more than* Parliaments; but, whatever may be the inclinations of the *govern-ments or* rulers for the time being, governments as such cannot and do *companies.* not take up enterprise for its own sake. Nor are companies formed to promote adventure, except so far as it is identified with commerce or with the extension of some branch of knowledge: their part is played later, when the pioneers have pointed the way, and when the work has become too extensive and too complicated to be left solely in individual hands. Consequently the question, How far has love of enterprise, apart from other motives, influenced colonisation? nearly means,

6   GEOGRAPHY OF THE COLONIES.

CHAPTER II.

Second motive, desire of wealth.

What part in colonising the world has been taken by the few great individual explorers?

4. The close connexion between the second motive, viz. desire of wealth, and colonisation, is clear enough to need but few words, Men being what they are, this motive must be present in every age and country, to any men or associations of men, who take part in colonising. And with states and governments it is all-powerful.

Love of adventure may overpower other motives in some minds, but very few characters are so constituted as to look only to the excitement which accompanies adventure or to the fame which follows it; and most men, however enterprising, aim at making a fortune as well as a name. The imaginations of the early Spanish adventurers were fired by reports of the treasures of the Indies; and the English sailors who followed in their track hoped to share the plunder, and to make their daring and their patriotism pay.

5. But, to contrast this commercial motive with mere love of adventure, its influence is specially noticeable in three tendencies. It has led to system and permanence in the world of colonising as opposed to single spasmodic efforts. It has in the second place made men co-operate and form companies for conquest or settlement. And thirdly it has determined the part taken by the state in colonisation.

6. The first point may be illustrated by reference to the voyages which have been made to the Arctic regions. The record of Arctic adventure consists of a number of more or less isolated attempts at exploration: and so far as any systematic work has been done in this direction, it has been done mainly with the view of discovering a North-West or North-East passage to the Indies, in other words of opening up a new road to commerce. If the climate of the Polar regions had been other than it is, and if, instead of icebound shores, explorers had found a land flowing with milk and honey, or even a practicable route for trade, it is clear that this

Commerce has led, 1. to system and permanence.

part of the earth's surface would not have been left deserted, but that a series of merchants and settlers would have followed in Frobisher's footsteps, and have permanently annexed this section of the New World. At the present time the only regular visitors to the Arctic regions are fishermen : and it is worth noticing that early colonisation, especially in North America, began in great measure with the pursuit of this branch of commerce.

While exploration was disjointed and irregular, the fishing trade could only be successfully carried on by a definite system, under which vessels were sent out to distinct destinations at fixed times. Thus regular intercourse was early established between Europe and North America. The men, who were engaged in the trade, were at once hardy and business-like, fit pioneers of sound colonisation. And the necessities of the traffic naturally led the peoples which were interested in it to win and keep a permanent hold on the shores visited.

It is interesting to bear in mind that, even at the present day, the French, who have lost all their possessions on the mainland of Canada, still retain some share in the fisheries which first attracted their merchant seamen to the North American coasts.

7. In order to produce system and permanence there must be co-operation. A house can only be built with the help of mortar to hold the bricks and stones together; and commerce has acted as the mortar, which has made it possible to utilise the disjointed stones of exploration in building up strong and lasting colonies.

2. Toformation of companies,

The part played by companies in colonising will be alluded to in a later chapter : here it is enough to take one illustration, and to point to the fact that English colonisation did not begin in earnest, until chivalry and knight-errantry had given way to the commercial spirit,[1] and until the daring

---

[1] See Doyle's 'History of the English in America,' vol. i. chap. vi.

explorers of the age of Elizabeth had been succeeded by prosaic business associations such as the Virginia and the East India companies.

3. to government taking part in colonisation.

8. And if this desire of wealth has led to the formation of colonising companies, it has also been the motive which beyond others has induced states and governments to take a direct part in conquest or settlement.

In taking and holding dependencies, a government looks to the material advantages to be derived from them either directly or indirectly: even if it plants a purely military post, its object in so doing is to protect and consolidate its resources.

In old days the dependencies of a state were, roughly speaking, either tributary peoples, paying an annual sum to their suzerain; such were the dependencies of Athens and Rome: or they were emporia of trade, such as the settlements formed by the Carthaginians. Again, when the governments of modern Europe took up the work of conquering and settling the New World, they aimed directly at adding to their material resources. In Professor Seeley's[1] words, 'what the state wanted was revenue, hence it became necessary to regard the new countries rather as so much wealth to be transported into Europe than as a new seat for European civilisation.'

And at the present day, if a nation annexes some new territory, though it does not look to a direct payment of gold and silver, yet its action is determined by the advantages which it hopes ultimately to reap in the way of trade. Such, to take one recent instance only, is the object aimed at in declaring an English protectorate over part of New Guinea; the step has been taken with a view to the future maintenance and development of Australian trade in the Southern seas.

Third motive, political and social discontent.

9. The third motive, political and social discontent, may in a sense be identified with desire of wealth, as most men who are dissatisfied with the government or social condition of

[1] 'Expansion of England,' Lecture IV.

MOTIVES OF COLONISATION. 9

their country, and leave home on that account, may be supposed to be desirous of bettering themselves. Still there is a real distinction between the political and social motive on the one hand and the commercial on the other. The latter is always at work; the former operates only at certain periods in a nation's history. The more prosperous a country is, the more active is the commercial spirit in it; whereas it is at times of depression and unhappiness that the motive of discontent is most powerfully felt. Desire of wealth influences all citizens alike, but discontent animates one section or class of the community as opposed to the others. And lastly political and social causes tend to take men entirely away from their old homes; while commerce, though it leads, as has been said, to permanent settlements in foreign parts, yet, in bringing about such settlements, regards them as essentially offshoots from, and feeders of, the mother country.

The Greek colonies proper, as opposed to the tributary dependencies of the Greek States, sprang mainly from political or social causes; from over-population with its necessary consequence of discontent; or from the struggles between the political parties in the various cities, the bitterness of which was intensified by the narrow space within which the contending parties were cooped up. And the colonies, which originated in this source, were permanent settlements in foreign and more or less distant countries, such as in Asia Minor or Sicily, and were from first to last absolutely independent of the mother state. The generic name ἀποικία indicates that the main object of the founders of Greek colonies was simply to get away from their old homes.

Again, the origin of the earliest permanent English settlement on the mainland of America, the Virginian colony, may be traced to social causes[1]: 'Virginia was the offspring

[1] Doyle's 'History of the English in America,' vol. i. chap. vi.

of economical distress as New England was of ecclesiastical conflicts.' And in our own time this same love of political or social independence is a most fruitful source of emigration; as may be seen in the case of the Irish, who seek to exchange English rule for that of the United States, and look for a part of the world where there will be no rent to pay and no eviction to fear; or in that of the Germans or the Basques, who leave their homes to escape the burden of military service.

Fourth motive, religion.

10. The connexion between religion and colonisation is a subject of the greatest historical interest; but only a few illustrations can here be given, to show how powerful the religious motive has been, and in what different ways it has operated.

Religion has led, 1. to exploration,

Colonisation includes exploration, conquest, and settlement: at each of these three stages religion has played an all-important part. It was the desire to promote the Christian faith, which stirred up the father of modern exploration, Prince Henry of Portugal, to send expeditions to search out the African coast. When Columbus turned his eyes to the New World, he had it in his mind to find a road to Jerusalem through the Indies and to lead a new Crusade. It was Champlain's aim, when exploring the backwoods of Canada, to work out the conversion of the Indian tribes and to open new fields for the spread of Christianity. And—to take one instance from later times—the life of Livingstone is a great record of missionary and explorer in one.

It is not wonderful that religion has been a fruitful parent of adventure. Men, who are fired by religious enthusiasm, think lightly of difficulties, which but for this impulse would be held insurmountable; and the work of exploring what is vague and unknown is in harmony with a strong sense of the supernatural. While too often, it must be allowed, the end has been made to justify the means, and the holiness of

MOTIVES OF COLONISATION.

their aims has made explorers conveniently blind to the nature of the intermediate steps.

11. After the explorer comes the conqueror, with the Cross or the Crescent for his banner; and religion is seen to be a powerful incentive to the annexation of the newly found territories and to the subjection of their savage inhabitants. The record of the Mohammedan invasions, of the Crusades, and of countless other struggles, each one more revolting than another, shows that, throughout history, religion and war have gone hand in hand, and shows further that the work of invaders and conquerors has never been so terribly thorough as when undertaken in the name of religion.

Among Christian sects, the Roman Catholic Church has in the past been the most militant and active. It has been better organised, more despotic, and perhaps more pliant than other religious bodies. And it may be that through its gorgeous ceremonial, it has been more successful than the less ostentatious Churches of Protestantism in impressing savage or half-civilised races, accustomed to associate religion with outward sights and sounds.

Towards the end of the Middle Ages its power was firmly established in Spain. In no country was its rule more implicitly obeyed; and in none were its outward symbols more imposing or its organisation more complete. Further, at the time when Columbus sailed on his first voyage, the war with the Moors in Spain had just been brought to a successful issue, the Christian had finally triumphed over the infidel at home, and the Spanish government was burning with a desire to extend the field of its religious conquests, so that 'they might always be occupied in bringing infidels to the knowledge of the Holy Catholic faith[1].'

This religious element in the history of the Spaniards in America must always be borne in mind. It recalls the story

CHAPTER II.

2. *to conquest.*

---

[1] See Helps' 'Spanish Conquest of America,' vol. i. bk. ii. chap. i.

CHAPTER II. of the conquest of Canaan by the Chosen People; and it helps to explain the daring of the conquerors, the interest taken in the work by the home government, and the rapidity and energy with which lands were conquered as soon as found, and natives claimed as subjects, as if they and theirs were the lawful inheritance of a Christian power.

But it was not only the warlike Catholics of Spain, who were devoured with zeal for the conversion of the heathen: a similar spirit animated at least to some extent the first English colonisers of America.

The Virginia[1] Company placed this object in the forefront of their scheme, combined missionary and mercantile enterprise, and secured money and friends for the purpose of spreading the Christian religion among the heathen. Protestants indeed have not always behaved less vigorously than Roman Catholics in the matter of conversion. In the case of Ceylon, for instance, the Dutch, in whom years of struggle with the Inquisition at home had bred a spirit of counter-bigotry, are known to have imposed their religion upon the natives in a more arbitrary fashion than the Roman Catholic Portuguese, whom they superseded[2].

12. In the work of conquest then, in East and West alike, the influence of religion was in old days thrown on the side of the conquerors, giving a sanction even to slavery as a means of saving souls. But when the European had taken possession of the land of the heathen and held the people in subjection, and when the triumph of Christianity was no longer in doubt, the ministers of religion as a rule used their power for a better purpose, to check the excesses of the conquerors and enforce humane treatment of the natives. Spanish priests and friars in the West Indies did not shrink from exposing and, as far as in them lay, restraining the cruelty of their fellow-countrymen; and Jesuits, Moravians,

---

[1] See Doyle, 'English in America,' vol. i. chap. vi. p. 217.
[2] See Emerson Tennant's 'Christianity in Ceylon,' chap. ii.

MOTIVES OF COLONISATION.

Quakers, and others stood out in the East and West alike as friends and champions of the native races, and won from them the love and honour which they well deserved. Yet even under these circumstances the religious motive did not work entirely for good. In its Roman Catholic dress, at any rate, it stood in various parts of the world utterly against our ideas of liberty and independence. It inculcated kindliness to the natives, but kindliness as to inferior beings. The Guaranis in the Jesuit missions[1] of Paraguay were humanely treated, but what we call manly self-reliance was banished from among them. And in the East, if the Portuguese missionaries and notably the Jesuits, following in the steps of St. Francis Xavier, did much towards humanising and educating the natives of India, they appear on the other side to have offered little opposition to the abuses of the civil government, and to have used the influence of the ecclesiastical hierarchy, which centred at Goa, to rivet still firmer the chains of despotic rule.

CHAPTER II.

13. Passing from exploration and conquest to settlement, religion is seen to have produced two distinct and almost opposite effects. On the one hand it has beyond all other causes led men to leave their homes and emigrate for good and all: on the other it has under certain circumstances proved a strong bond between the colony and the mother-country.

3. *to settlement.*

A good instance of the first effect is found in the emigration of the Huguenots from France to England, the Netherlands, and other Protestant parts of Europe, in consequence of the revocation of the edict of Nantes. The result of the persecution of the Protestants by the Catholic government of France was, that a large number of French citizens, preferring their religious belief to riches and even to home and country, permanently settled beyond the French borders,

In some cases it has been a barrier between the mother country and the colony.

[1] An account of these missions will be found in Helps' 'Spanish Conquest of America,' and in Watson's 'History of Spanish and Portuguese South America during the Colonial Period.' See also Merivale's 'Lectures on Colonisation.'

and gradually became incorporated with foreign communities. This was a case of a body of people flying for refuge from persecution to neighbouring and civilised countries. The planting of the New England colonies, on the other hand, shows religion as having been sufficiently powerful to induce men to go forth into the wilderness, to an almost unknown world, and there to found a wholly new society, wherein to worship in quietness the God of their fathers[1]. The Puritan settlers in New England were in great measure well-to-do men; they did not leave their homes on account of poverty. Nor was the land in which they settled one of great commercial promise. They left England mainly on religious grounds, and made up their minds to live and die in distant exile, because they feared God more than man.

In others it has been a link between them.

In these cases, as in many others, religion has been a separating force: but it may prove and often has proved a connecting link. For instance, almost the only tie between the Greek colonies and their mother-cities was a religious tie. The sacred fire was brought from the parent state to the colony, and at the public festivals and sacrifices due honour was paid by the colonists to the city from which they or their fathers had emigrated, but to which they owed no political allegiance.

Again, one of the few bonds which kept the Spanish American colonies so long attached to Spain, in spite of the distance, the weakness, and the misgovernment of the mother-country, was the influence of the Roman Catholic Church.

And if it was difference of religion which drove the Pilgrim Fathers from England to America, it may be said, on the other hand, that a general harmony in religious feeling has remained to this day as one among many links between Great Britain and the United States.

---

[1] Compare Seeley, 'Expansion of England,' Lecture VIII.

CHAPTER III.

CLIMATE AND RACE.

1. COLONISATION implies a place to be colonised and a people to colonise; and the good or ill success of colonies depends mainly on two factors, climate and race.

Different climates suit different races.

Different races are of course suited to different climates. The negro thrives in a hot moist climate—on the coast of Guinea or in the West Indies; but he has no place in the colder zones. 'Instead of deriving firmness and activity from the cold, he becomes inert, sluggish and languid[1];' and so in Africa his home is between the tropics; and in the United States, while three-fifths of the whole population of South Carolina (according to the 1880 census), and more than one-half of that of Louisiana and Mississippi, are coloured, in the states of Maine, New York, or Massachusetts, the proportion of negroes to whites is less than two per cent.

The white man, on the contrary, has been set by nature in temperate latitudes; his bodily physique and his character alike deteriorate in the tropics; and if he be transplanted to some other climate than his own, experience has shown that he will bear a change to greater cold better than to greater heat.

---

[1] Bryan Edwards, 'History of West Indies,' bk. iv. chap. v. He is speaking of the condition of the negro in the chill of the morning. A colony of rebel slaves or Maroons from Jamaica was planted in Nova Scotia in 1795, but in 1800 they were removed to Sierra Leone—too soon to judge of the effects of the climate upon them.

CHAPTER III.

French and English emigrants, for instance, have thriven far more amid the snows of Canada than in the tropical West Indian islands. And a comparison of the branches of the European race, which have sent settlers to America, shows that, in the first instance, the Spaniards and Portuguese from the warm South of Europe settled and took root in Central and South America, whereas the French and English planted themselves mainly in the more northerly and colder part of the continent; and that, at the present day, the Italians head the list of immigrants into South America, while the Germans, Swedes, and Norwegians stream into the Northern districts of the United States.

Different climates lead to different dependencies of the same people.

2. And as different temperatures suit different races, so, to take the case of a single colonising people, it is this element of climate, which has mainly determined what kinds of colonies or dependencies have been formed in various quarters of the world.

A nation may explore or conquer in any climate, but it can make its home in some climates only, not in others. An Englishman's constitution may be able to stand a voyage to the North Pole on the one hand, or an expedition into the heart of the Soudan on the other; but Englishmen could not thrive, and breed, and bring up healthy children, either far within the Arctic circle or in Equatorial Africa or India. Consequently the differences in kind in the English dependencies vary in great measure with the differences in climate.

Compare, for instance, three different parts of the English empire: the West Africa Settlements, India, and Australia. West Africa is a part of the world where, on account of climatic causes, it is almost impossible for an Englishman to take up his residence for any length of time without injury to his health; it has been found necessary to grant leave of absence to the civil officers in the service at more frequent intervals than in the case of other tropical or semi-tropical dependencies, and to send them constantly to Madeira or to

CLIMATE AND RACE.

England for change of air; and no white troops are employed on the coast, which is garrisoned by the coloured West India regiments[1]. In short, experience has shown that the average Englishman not only cannot make his home in West Africa, but cannot live there at all for any prolonged time; and English colonisation in this part of the world amounts to nothing more than keeping a supervision over a certain part of the fever-stricken West African coast, for purposes partly commercial, partly philanthropic.

As compared with Sierra Leone and the Gold Coast, India has a climate fairly healthy for Europeans: consequently it can be garrisoned to a great extent by English troops; and Englishmen can live in the country, engage in trade, and practise their professions for years at a time, without materially suffering in health. But here again there is a limit: hardly any Englishman can settle down in India for a perpetuity; English children, born in the hot climate of the East, deteriorate in morale and physique unless they are sent to Europe at a certain age; and if a man goes out from England to India, he does so meaning to come home sooner or later. Consequently, while the English have been able for generations to hold India as a military dependency, and have not been compelled to content themselves with a few isolated positions, or an indefinite protectorate along the coast, but have established a system of order and administration throughout the length and breadth of the great peninsula; yet the greater part of India is not, and, as far as can be judged, never will be a home for Englishmen.

The case of Australia is widely different. Here, except in the tropical northern districts, the English race can find a permanent resting-place. Consequently there is a constant stream of emigration flowing from Great Britain to the Australian colonies; a new England is springing up at the Antipodes; English farmers are planted throughout the

[1] They are of course officered by Englishmen.

CHAPTER III.

A race to colonise must have 1. a strong physique and power of expansion.

country; and towns like Sydney and Melbourne reproduce to the full the vigour and activity of our own great cities.

3. It is clear then that climate decides where a race can and where it cannot endure. But, for colonising, a race requires certain special qualifications; and, as these qualifications are not found all combined in a single breed, it follows that differences in national character, like differences in climate, have led and will lead to the formation of various kinds of dependencies.

A race, to be able to colonise, must in the first place be one of strong physique, multiplying and reproductive, formed by nature to spread and expand over a larger area than its original home.

Taking in this connexion the broadest division of mankind, it is seen that the white race, which in historical times has done by far the most colonising work in the world, possesses apparently greater stamina and more power of expansion than the coloured races. Though it does not thrive in some climates as it does in others, yet there is hardly any part of the world where it has not secured and maintained some kind of foothold. Europe has for many generations overflowed into the other continents, whereas the coloured races make little or no show in Europe. The negro remains within certain limits even in Africa: and the Chinese, who are far the strongest and the most expansive of the non-Aryan races, and who seem to be in great measure impervious to the effects of climate, have as yet (partly no doubt from political causes) but touched upon the borders of the white man's new home in California and the Australian colonies.

Among the branches of the white race again, the inhabitants of Great Britain distinctly come first in the field of colonisation; and, as Professor Seeley has pointed out, one great speciality of the English people, as far as modern history is concerned, has been 'unparallelled expansion[1].'

[1] 'Expansion of England,' part ii. Lecture VIII, end.

CLIMATE AND RACE.

It would be superfluous to multiply illustrations of this well-known fact. Between 1851 and 1881 the population of England and Wales rose from 18 millions to 26 millions: at the same time (between the years 1853 and 1883) nearly 1,400,000 English and Welsh emigrated to the United States alone[1]. Year after year the area of English colonisation has been widening in Canada, in Australia, and in South Africa. And a reference to the last census of the United States will show how the English-speaking race, which a hundred years ago was to be found only along the Atlantic coast[2], has now spread from sea to sea.

4. In addition to physical endurance and reproductive power, however, there are some more special colonising qualities to be noticed.

Colonisation, as has been seen, includes exploration, conquest and settlement. A colonising race, therefore, may be expected to have one or more of the following characteristics; to be enterprising, commercial, inclined to emigrate and form new settlements, to be a warlike and conquering race, to be able to assimilate with other races, and, lastly, to be able to govern. And according as different qualities have predominated in a particular race or nationality, so its part in the history of colonisation will be found to bear a special impress.

CHAPTER III.

2. Certain special qualities. Six characteristics of colonising races.

5. To take the first of these six characteristics. A mixed race is usually progressive and enterprising.

Compare the English and Chinese, the former a breed composed of various elements, the latter comparatively pure and unalloyed. The English have, as the saying is, moved with the age, and adapted themselves to change of time and circumstance. The Chinese, on the contrary, while they have

1. Enterprise. Mixed breeds are enterprising.

---

[1] Excluding Scotch and Irish: the figures are taken from the 'Statesman's Year Book.'
[2] See the United States census for 1880. This is a splendid publication, showing by a series of maps the progress of population since the first census, taken in 1790.

CHAPTER III.

multiplied and emigrated, have yet remained for centuries in the same intellectual groove: their government is at present as pedantic as ever it was; their mode of administration and their forms of justice remain unchanged. If they do not exclude foreigners, it is only because they have been forced to admit them; and the presence of Europeans in China has had little effect upon the ways and customs of the people. In 1876 a railway was laid by a European company for a few miles from Shanghai; but it had not been working many months, when it was bought up and taken over by the Chinese government, and the lines were torn up again.

Or take the case of Spain. At the end of the 15th and the beginning of the 16th centuries, the Spaniards were, with the Portuguese, the most forward and enterprising people in Europe. They are now among the most backward and reactionary of European nations. The Spanish breed was originally a very mixed one: Iberians, Celts, Phoenicians, Romans, Goths, Vandals, and Moors contributed to it. But, as soon as the nation really came into existence, a policy of exclusion was begun, and was thenceforward steadily carried on. Men with new and progressive ideas were proscribed, heretics were stamped out, Jews were expelled, the Moors were driven out wholesale, and at the present day Spain contains fewer residents of foreign birth than most other countries of Europe. So it would seem that, as the country became more exclusive and the breed less alloyed, the spirit of enterprise gradually died away[1].

As also maritime peoples.

6. As a seagoing race is ever enterprising and adventurous, and as the ocean is the great high road between the various parts of the earth, the work of colonisation both in ancient and modern ages has been carried on mainly by the sea: and but few colonising peoples, from the time of the Phoenicians to that of the English, have been outside the

[1] The 'Statesman's Year Book' says that, according to the 1877 census, there were then only 26,834 resident foreigners in Spain.

category of maritime nations. It is true that the great movements of barbarians from Asia to Europe; and invasions, such as those of the Saracens and Turks, may be given as instances of migration by land: but transplantations of whole races, and great waves of invasion, can hardly be classed under the head of colonisation; and at any rate it may be safely said that, with two exceptions, the peoples of Europe have colonised by sea rather than by land; those exceptions being two great military nations, viz. the Romans in ancient times and the Russians in our own.

7. There is no feature more striking in the history of colonisation than the amount of work done by small nations, as for instance the Phoenicians, the Greeks, the Portuguese, the Dutch, and others.

And small states.

This has been in part due to the element of restlessness, arising from over-population; but it has also been the result of the vigour and independence, which so often characterizes small states, and which leads naturally to emigration and the formation of colonies. The life of little communities is in many respects more vigorous than that of great empires: where the area of the country is limited and the population small, each individual is of importance, and takes an active part in public life; whereas in a great nation single citizens are too often lost in the mass and never develop independence of thought and action.

To take one instance only; individual life had far more play in the little States of ancient Greece, than can possibly be the case in the large nationalities of the present day; consequently the single city of Athens produced a series of great men which perhaps has never been equalled; and the influence of Greek character, Greek literature, and Greek art on the world in general has been out of all proportion to the numbers of the Greek race and the size of their communities.

8. It is a sign of an enterprising race to owe its colonies to private effort, independent of the state. At the outset of modern

CHAPTER III.

The most successful colonisers have been the least State-ridden.

colonisation, Spanish, Portuguese, and French explorers were individually at least as daring and as adventurous as English: but the ordinary Spaniard or Portuguese or Frenchman had not the same power of private initiative as the ordinary Englishman. And if the work done by the English nation has in the end proved to be of better quality and more lasting character, than that of other peoples; if the English succeeded in India, while the Portuguese failed; if British America has prospered, while Spanish America has not; if the United States grew and developed out of all proportion to the French colony in Canada; one great reason for the difference seems to be, that the members of the English-speaking race, as compared with other races, have throughout its history, both at home and abroad, relied not so much on their government as on themselves.

2. Aptitude for trading.

9. But little need be said of the commercial spirit to supplement the allusions made to it in the last chapter. Commerce, it has been seen, as opposed to adventure pure and simple, tends to forming permanent colonies. The Phoenicians, the Carthaginians, and the Greeks, in ancient times stand out as instances of trading peoples which have colonised; while modern history points to the Portuguese, the Dutch, and the English.

Trading on a large scale must be carried on by means of companies: and it is worth noticing that, while the Spaniards up to a certain point, and the Portuguese in a far greater degree, could lay claim to being placed in the list of commercial peoples, they did not adopt the system of chartered companies[1], which was so universal among the Dutch and English, but allowed the Crown to be the great monopolist. In other words history shows that the trader spirit has not been so deeply implanted in the Latin as in the Teuton races; and if the Dutch and English have borne the

---

[1] The Portuguese government, however, as shown elsewhere, in later years gave charters to companies in connexion with Brazil.

impress of merchants to a greater extent than their southern rivals, certainly as colonisers they can show a more successful record.

10. But a people or race may be commercial, without being inclined permanently to emigrate and settle away from home. The Dutch are a case in point. Though their country is small, they have not felt the pressure of overpopulation: consequently while they have formed and held colonies, and have from time to time sent out a certain number of emigrants, as for instance to South Africa and the United States, they have not been a settling race to the same extent as some other European peoples[1]: and considering what a high place they have taken among colonising nations, they have done singularly little in leavening the population of the world.

The Spaniards in Central and South America, the English in North America and Australasia, the Germans and Irish in the United States, are instances of races which have shown a readiness to go out from the land of their fathers, and to make their homes in a foreign country. Of course at any given time there must be some particular motive to induce people to emigrate, as has been seen in the last chapter; but, independently of special causes which operate at special times, some races have clearly proved themselves to be more ready than others to leave home, and, having left, to be less inclined to return. Not that such peoples are more restless or less homeloving than others: no one would accuse the Germans of being indifferent to their fatherland, or the English of being a nomad and homeless race: but they have the strength to carry their homes and associations with them across the seas; and rather to widen the original area of their respective nationalities, than to lose themselves in foreign lands.

3. Readiness to emigrate.

---

[1] This is pointed out in Heeren's 'Political System of Europe and its Colonies,' Tr. vol. i. par. 1, p. 1: in Merivale's 'Lectures on Colonisation,' Lecture II, etc.

CHAPTER III.

4. Capacity for fighting.

11. It has been pointed out, however, that people rarely if ever settle in an absolutely uninhabited country: and this is especially true in these later days, when most of the good land in the world has been already occupied. Consequently we look for colonising races to have the further qualities which have been enumerated: they should be able to fight and conquer, to assimilate with others, and to govern.

A race may be a colonising race, in the sense of emigrating and settling, without having any element of the conqueror in it. The Chinese and the Jews, for intance, have emigrated in numbers to foreign countries, and the latter at any rate have, beyond all races, made their home in other lands than their own: but there have been practically no Chinese or Jewish colonies, in the sense that there have been Greek or Spanish or English, i.e. in the sense of distinct settlements, planted either as independent states or as dependencies of the mother country.

All the great colonising peoples, in the ordinary sense of the word, except perhaps the Phœnicians, have had some conquering instinct in them. Even the Greeks, who formed isolated settlements rather than colonial empires, and who were utterly weakened by subdivision into small states, showed by their history—a history of constantly successful struggle against overwhelmingly larger numbers of barbarian foes—that they knew how to fight and conquer if not how to govern. And even the Dutch, who were in character unaggressive traders, became in the course of their history one of the first military nations in the world; and their descendants, the South African Boers, have but lately given evidence of having inherited fine fighting qualities.

5. Power of assimilation.

12. Conquest however is a temporary matter only; the colonisation of an uninhabited country may begin with conquering, but it requires in addition some element of greater permanence. This is found in the two remaining characteristics of colonising races, power of assimilation, and capacity for

government. It is not difficult for a strong nation to subdue a savage tribe or people: the difficulty comes later and consists in finding a *modus vivendi* between the conquerors and the conquered. It is comparatively easy to extend English conquests in South Africa, and annex fresh square miles of territory; but the difficulty of teaching English, Dutch, and natives to live side by side has at present proved almost insurmountable. Here then a race which can adapt itself to others has a great advantage; while even at the earlier, the conquering stage, the power of assimilation has been shown in history to be of the greatest value.

The Spaniards, for instance, were notably helped in their conquest of America by the facility with which they intermixed with the natives; and it is matter of story how much Cortes was helped in his Mexican campaigns by his Indian mistress and interpreter Marina[1].

The French afford a still more striking instance of the influence which attaches to a race, ready to adopt the customs and manners of the natives of the country, or to find means of engrafting upon the latter their own civilisation. In Canada, we read of Champlain spending his life in great measure in the Indian lodges; and of a later French governor, de Frontenac, taking part in the savage rites of the Indians, and joining in the war dance. And in the East Indies, when French and English were striving for the mastery, Dupleix not only converted himself for the time being into an Oriental prince, but achieved the more difficult feat of habituating the natives to the discipline and drill of European soldiers, showing thereby the way by which a few Europeans might conquer and hold a great Eastern empire[2].

---

[1] See Prescott's 'Conquest of Mexico.'
[2] See what is said on this point in Seeley's 'Expansion of England,' Part ii. Lecture III. The success of the East India Company was largely due in parts of India to intermarriage of officials with native ladies. See Meadows Taylor's Life.

CHAPTER III.

Among ancient peoples the Greeks were pre-eminent for power of assimilation[1]: and Juvenal's well-known line reminds us that they became a proverb for their power of accommodating themselves to all conditions of life. They were also equally successful in impressing their influence on other countries and races. While the Romans became politically the masters of the ancient world, 'Victorious Rome,' to quote Gibbon's words adapted from Horace, 'was herself subdued by the arts of Greece'[2]. And throughout Eastern Europe, in Asia Minor, in Syria and in Egypt, the Greek language, Greek manners and Greek civilisation held the field.

In modern Europe the Latin races have clearly shown, in settling as in conquering, that they possess this quality to a greater extent than the Teuton. Indeed the English difficulties in South Africa may be traced in no small degree to want of capacity for assimilation on the part of the English and Dutch races.

But there is a possible drawback to this power of assimilation: it lies in this, that the colonising race may in time be merged in the lower native race, and become degraded in its new home. This has been the case with the Spanish in America: the Spaniard has in course of years rather become assimilated to the Indian than the Indian to the Spaniard; a mixed race has sprung up of lower type than that of the original immigrant; and the final result, as seen in the South American states, compares unfavourably with that which has been produced in other cases, where the incoming race has, as in North America, shown less adaptability to and less inclination to mix with the native inhabitants of the country.

6. *Capacity for ruling.*

13. The last and most important characteristic to be looked for in colonising races is the power of governing. It is a quality which would seem to be found more especially among peoples which are deficient in capacity for assimilation; a ruler must

---

[1] 'Graeculus esuriens ad caelum, jusseris, ibit.'
[2] Chapter II.

possess strength of character, and strength of character is not often compatible with flexibility. The Romans in ancient, the English in modern times stand out above all peoples for having built up and maintained a great empire of Colonies and dependencies. There was little power of assimilation in the Romans, and there is little in the English; but in the character of both nations might be traced a strong leaning to system, a strong love of justice and law, and some idea of governing for the sake of the governed.

Aristotle says of the Spartans that 'warring was their salvation but governing their ruin'[1]. These words apply to many nations which have once been great, and the secret of whose decay has been their inability to rule. They are eminently true of half-barbaric races like the Turks; and they might be written on the title-page of Spanish and Portuguese history. Colonising on any large scale must imply dealing with subject races; and the past has shown that, in spite of other defects, the people which can govern will in the end prevail.

[1] Politics, ii. 9, ἐσώζοντο μὲν πολεμοῦντες ἀπώλλυντο δὲ ἄρξαντες.

CHAPTER IV.

MODES OF COLONISING AND KINDS OF COLONISTS.

CHAPTER IV.

Three modes of colonising.
1. *By individuals, they have generally been protected by the state.*

1. Colonisation can be carried out by individual men apart from the state, by the state itself, or by private enterprise aided by the state.

There is no need to repeat examples of the first of these three methods of colonising. Many instances might be given, such as the ancient Greek colonies, the earliest of the Puritan settlements in America, and others. But it is worth while to point out that in any case there must be some association of persons to make a colony; and that, when companies have been deliberately formed to promote a scheme of colonisation, they have generally, if not always, been to some extent protected and privileged by the state. While Robinson Crusoe lived alone, and even after he was joined by Friday, he can scarcely be said to have colonised his island. Colonisation began with the arrival of the Spaniards, and of Will Atkins and his comrades. Here there was no deliberate formation of a colonising company: if there had been, Crusoe would probably have sought and obtained a charter from the English government: and, even as things were, supposing the romance to have been turned into history, Crusoe's island would doubtless soon have come under the wing of the state.

The mutineers of the Bounty who settled in Pitcairn island, may be quoted as an instance of deliberate colonisation, unaided by the state. But in the first place it is clear that this settlement was far removed from a carefully planned, businesslike scheme of colonising; and in the second place it will be remembered that as years have gone on, the Pitcairn islanders have received at least indirect encouragement and protection from the English government.

The Welsh settlement on the Chupat river in Patagonia is an interesting example of voluntary association of private individuals for purposes of colonisation. Yet even in this scheme the signs of state interference have been clear and unmistakeable[1]. The promoters obtained permission from the government of the Argentine republic to plant a colony within their borders: the settlers received formal grants of land, and, at the outset, pecuniary assistance from that government: and of late years the district has been brought more directly under the supervision of the Argentine authorities. Further, the visits, which have been periodically paid to the colony by one or other of H. M. ships, have shown the interest hitherto taken by the English government in a body of settlers who have gone out from Great Britain.

2. The second mode of colonisation, viz. directly by the state, needs also no special illustration. It has been seen that among some races Government is more ubiquitous than among others. And it is clear, that in any case of a colonial empire, of a system in which colonies proper and subject dependencies are intermixed, much must be due to the direct action of the state in securing the possessions in the first instance, and still more in subsequently consolidating and ruling them. To take examples from the English empire only; the government of this country acquired Canada by force of arms, it occupied Cyprus under

---

[1] Reference to the founding of this settlement in 1865 is made in the report on the Argentine Republic for 1865 made by Mr. Ford, then Secretary of legation at Buenos Ayres, and dated 30 Oct. 1866. It was presented to Parliament in 1867. Periodical reports on this settlement are forwarded to the Admiralty by the commanders of the ships sent to visit it.

CHAPTER IV.

3. *By chartered companies.*

treaty with another government, and it secured Australia by planting in it a purely state colony.

3. There remains the third mode of colonisation, in which the work is done by private individuals, deliberately assisted by government. Such assistance has usually taken the form of granting monopolies of land or trade. Charters have been given sometimes to one or more proprietors, as in the case of Lord Baltimore or William Penn, proprietors of Maryland and Pennsylvania respectively: sometimes to a company, such as the Virginia or East India company. Companies of this kind, as has been seen, played comparatively little part in Spanish or Portuguese colonisation; whereas the history of the Dutch and English in the East is in great measure the history of the Dutch and English East India companies, a history showing how a body of merchants can develop into conquerors and rulers.

The object with which such companies are formed, is of course mainly commercial. Consequently any colonising work done by them is likely to be sound, systematic, and practical, directed almost entirely to making a profit. They are not liable like individual men to have their operations interrupted by death[1]; and they run less risk than the state of being taken in by their agents, partly because they keep a sharper eye on their own interests, partly because to cheat government has for some reason or other always been considered to be less criminal than to cheat private employers. On the other hand a company as such has little or no conscience. In its dealings with natives the idea of governing for the sake of the governed is as a rule but faintly present; and men of the type of Clive and Warren Hastings find that all lofty schemes of government and empire must give way to the one main object of getting good dividends for the shareholders. Companies can explore,

[1] This is clearly pointed out as to the East India Company in Ransome's lectures on 'our colonies and India,' Lecture III.

trade, and conquer with success, but the work of governing finds out their weak points; and Adam Smith's verdict upon them is, that 'the government of an exclusive company of merchants is perhaps the worst of all governments for any country whatever'[1].

CHAPTER IV.

4. The material out of which a colony is formed, i.e. its population, consists of natives, where there are native inhabitants, as is usually the case; and of immigrants.

Classes of inhabitants in a colony.

If the number of natives is largely in excess of that of the immigrants, the result is a subject dependency. If the native element is insignificant, the community approaches more and more nearly to a colony proper.

1. *natives.*

The position, which the natives hold, depends partly on themselves, partly on the incoming people. Their own breed may be physically weak, incapable of amalgamating, and, when brought into contact with a higher race, doomed to stand still if not to decay. Such seems to be the case with the North American Indians. Or they may be a strong breed, like the negro or Chinese, holding their own with the white man, even if they do not adapt themselves to his civilisation. On the other hand, the treatment of the native by the immigrant race will vary with the national character of the latter, with the institutions and form of government under which it has been trained, and with the time at which the immigration takes place. The history of colonisation shows the native races in almost every kind of status: as slaves pure and simple; such was their condition in the West Indies and in Brazil, in the early days of Spanish and Portuguese invasion: as minors in the eye of the law[2]; this was the position assigned by the Spanish government to its American subjects: as possessed of full civil but of few or no political rights; this is the case with the millions of

Causes which lead to their good or bad treatment.

---

[1] 'Wealth of Nations,' chapter on 'Causes of prosperity of new colonies.'
[2] See the references given on this point in chap. vi.

Hindoos and Tamils, who are under the British government! and finally as taking their place, like the New Zealand Maoris, in a representative colonial parliament.

In considering the treatment of natives in countries where white men have established themselves, it is not easy to say that one European people has shown itself to be more cruel by nature than another. The worst cruelties of the Spaniards were at times rivalled by the atrocities recorded of English adventurers; and the Spanish government was notably humane in its regulations for the protection of the Indians.

But it can safely be said that the spirit of humanity has grown faster in one nation than in another. The English of the present generation would not tolerate bull-baiting at home or slavery in the colonies; whereas our grandfathers flocked to bull-baits and to cock-fights, made large fortunes out of slave plantations, and looked on the slave trade as a legitimate branch of business.

Further, the sense of justice and law, which seems to be more ingrained in some races than in others, gradually reappears in the new country among the emigrants from the old. This sense is nurtured or repressed by the institutions under which a people has grown up: and therefore the treatment which is dealt out to the native races, with which the colonists come into contact, depends in great measure upon the nature of these institutions.

If a race has long been habituated to despotism, its members are more likely to tyrannise in their turn than the citizens of a self-governing state: and men who have been trained to responsibility at home are best fitted to exercise rule abroad. It seems hard to suppose that a Spaniard, brought up under the government of Philip the Second, could be a respecter of the rights and liberties and privileges of other men to the same extent as a follower of Pym and Hampden.

There is always a danger, however, in a subject dependency with a large native population, that the dominant minority of the foreign race, backed as they are by the strength of the mother country, will lose to some extent their respect for law and justice. And they need for a while at least to be held in check by the home government.

Englishmen in England are among equals: they are no better and no worse than their neighbours of the same breed and colour. In the East, on the contrary, they are recognised by the natives as a ruling caste; they are expected to command, and find that they are implicitly obeyed. Under such circumstances it is impossible that a consciousness of physical and moral superiority should not breed a certain amount of arrogance, and that the Englishman in India should not be more overbearing than he is at home.

The safeguard of native races, then, in a colonial empire, the centre of which is far distant from the outlying provinces, is found in the existence of a strong public opinion at home, and in the retention by the home government of the power to protect their native subjects, equally with their own citizens, until the time has come for the two classes to be placed on the same footing. In South Africa, it has been found more to the interest of the native races to keep their special districts under Imperial control, in certain cases, than to hand them over to a colonial government. And in the East, where settlers are few and natives are many, the English possessions are all Crown colonies, and the administration is directed and controlled from home.

5. There are, or have been in the past, three divisions of the immigrant population in colonies:—free settlers; slaves (a class now nearly extinct in European colonies); and those settlers, whose position is one of more or less modified dependence, such as convicts on the one hand, and indentured coolies on the other.

Three classes of immigrants.

CHAPTER IV.

1st class. Free settlers.

6. In considering the first class, it must be remembered that, especially in conquered dependencies, the free immigrants are often only temporary residents, partly civil and military officers, partly merchants and professional men, who have come to the colony for a term of years only, long or short as the case may be: and also that in all colonies containing a native population there arises, as years go on, a class of citizens formed by the intermixture of the incomers and the natives—a class, which in some countries, as for instance in parts of South America, eventually becomes a most important element in the community[1].

And even if temporary residents and half-breeds be excluded, it is difficult to make such a classification of the free settlers in a colony, as will serve any useful purpose.

They may be classified on the basis of Heeren's division of colonies.

Heeren[2] divides colonies into four classes, *agricultural, plantation, mining,* and *trading* colonies.

This division is hardly applicable to colonies at the present day. It would, for instance, be difficult to place any one of the Australian colonies under a single heading. Judged by her chief export, wool, Victoria is a pastoral colony: but the amount of gold raised from her mines places her at the same time high in the list of mining colonies: and the fact that half the Victorian population lives in the towns entitles her to a front place as a trading colony. If New South Wales is rich in flocks and herds, she is rich also in coal and other mineral. And Queensland adds sugar plantations to pastoral and mining industries.

But if the list is hardly a satisfactory classification of colonies, it serves as a description, though not an exhaustive one, of the different kinds of colonist.

[1] The 'Mestizoes' or Spanish Indian half-breeds, form a large proportion of the South American population, varying in the different states, but it is difficult to find any accurate figures on the subject.
[2] 'Political System of Europe and its Colonies:' chapter on Origin of Colonies.

Where colonisation has been uniform and systematic, spreading gradually through the new country, along its rivers and channels of communication; not massing the population in large numbers at a few points only, nor on the other hand allowing the families to straggle out of reach of one another; there it may be taken that the settlers are agriculturists of the type of the New England farmers.

Chapter IV. Agriculturists.

7. Planters on the other hand settle on large estates, more or less isolated from each other, employing capital and labour (till of late mainly slave labour) on a large scale, in producing articles of export for foreign markets: such are the coffee and tea planters of India and Ceylon, the sugar planters of the West Indies, or the cotton growers of the Southern states of America.

Planters.

The *pastoral* class is not specified in Heeren's list; and yet the members of this class play an important part in the colonisation of new countries, as the Australian sheep farmers, for instance, or the owners of cattle ranches in Texas. They live at least as isolated a life as the planters; but, not requiring to command the same amount of labour, they do not contribute, as large plantations do, to bring about an oligarchical state of society.

Sheep and cattle farmers.

Plantation life is the extreme of country life; the opposite pole is found in mining colonies, where the miners are European colonists or the descendants of Europeans. In them, population gathers densely at a few spots, in the midst, it may be, of a wilderness; the life is rather town than country life; the growth of numbers[1] is at a rate unknown in the more steady-going agricultural colonies; and the character of the colonists, as compared with that of the farmer or planter, is restless, pushing, and democratic.

Miners.

8. The report of the last (1880) census of the United

---

[1] Heeren remarks on mining colonies that 'they cannot as mere mining colonies ever attain to much population,' but his words apply to the Peruvian mines worked in old days by forced labour.

States will well illustrate the different growth of population in agricultural and mining districts. In the more agricultural state of Utah, the spread is shown to be steady and uniform; while in Colorado the discovery of mineral wealth brings a sudden influx of population. Similarly the discovery of the gold mines in Victoria brought about a sudden increase in the rate, and a change in the distribution and the character of the population, making this the most thickly populated and the most democratic part of Australia. In Brazil, the mining provinces have attracted the largest numbers, and, at any rate in past years, the most resolute and turbulent members of the community. And in South Africa, the discovery of the diamond fields has reared a large and populous town in the midst of a dusty desert.

Traders. The term 'trader' is so wide as to include the most opposite elements of society. Under this head may be gathered, on the one hand, merchants, who centre in the towns, and townspeople generally; and, on the other, roving dealers, who, like the fur-traders of Canada in old days, have no fixed abode, but spend their lives on or beyond the borders of the settlements. Traders are found everywhere, in the heart of central Africa as in the heart of London: but, as specimens of trading colonies, Heeren would presumably have instanced the Carthaginian depôts, planted in old days on the Western coasts of the Mediterranean. And, in the present century, such a station as Hongkong may, apart from its military character, well be styled a trading colony; it has no agricultural or mining or plantation resources of its own, but owes its prosperity entirely to the vast trade between China and Europe, which passes through its port.

The classes of free colonist might be indefinitely multiplied and subdivided; and it might be pointed out at length, how one kind of settler is to be found in one climate and soil rather than in another, as for instance the planters and their products belong specially to tropical or sub-tropical regions;

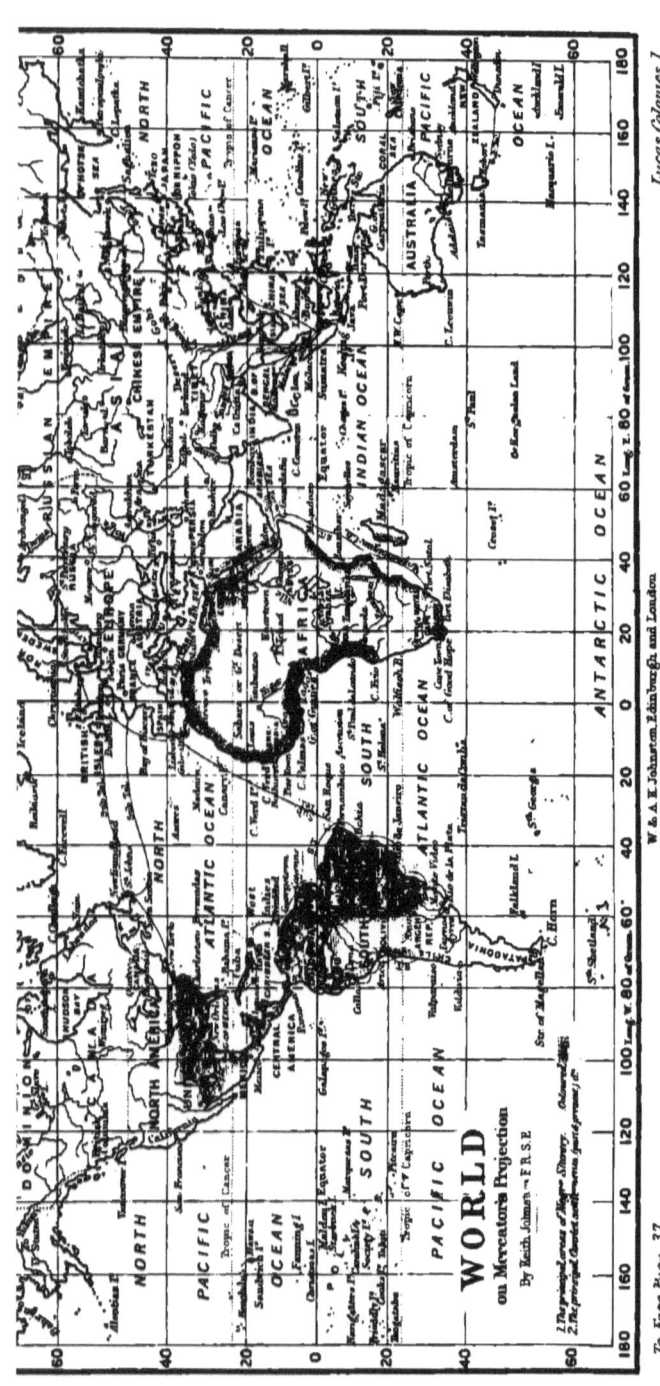

WORLD on Mercator's Projection
By Keith Johnson F.R.S.E.

W. & A. K. Johnston, Edinburgh and London

To Face Page 37. Lucas Colonies I.

COLONISING AND COLONISTS. 37

and how a particular race is better adapted to one kind of occupation than to another, as the French are said to have shown special aptitude for petty retail trading[1]. But in the present sketch it is impossible to lay down any very definite limits, or to do more than suggest certain well-known types of colonist and phases of colonisation.

CHAPTER IV.

9. Until quite lately slaves formed a most important element in the population of colonies. Ancient society was based on slavery. The so-called democracies of the old world were really oligarchies, the slaves as a rule far out-numbering the free citizens; and the institution of slavery was considered an inevitable consequence of political and social life. In the Middle Ages again villeins and serfs formed a large proportion of the population; and, to quote Hallam's words[2], "in every age and country, until times comparatively recent, personal servitude appears to have been the lot of a large, perhaps the greater, portion of mankind." It was left, however, to the nations of modern Europe to mark out a special race to be enslaved; to introduce and develop negro slavery; to import Africans into their colonies, as being better material for labour in the mines or on the plantations than the native inhabitants; and to treat the slave-trade as a valuable branch of commerce, a monopoly to be competed for by the most civilised nations of the day, and, as in the case of the Assiento compact, to be solemnly recognised in treaties[3].

2nd class. Slaves.

The slave-trade was instituted to supply labour to the West not to the East: and negro slavery has always been connected with the European colonies in the New World,

---

[1] This is remarked on in Burke's 'European Settlements in America,' published anonymously in 1757. See the reference in Merivale's 'Lectures on Colonisation and Colonies,' Lecture II.
[2] 'Middle Ages,' chap. ii. part ii.
[3] The Assiento or contract signed in 1713 between England and Spain gave England the exclusive right of importing negroes into the Spanish Indies.

rather than with their settlements in the old. Further, the system was called for, and prospered, only in the tropical, or at least the hotter, parts of America; in the Southern states of North America, in South America, and in the West Indies.

The plantation colonies were those in which slaves were most numerous and where the system was most fully developed. The negro labourer was found to be stronger than the native; and, coming from tropical Africa, he was able to work in a climate, in which the physique of the white man deteriorated. Slave labour too was adapted to the cultivation of the plantation products, tobacco, cotton, sugar and others, which required quantity of labour rather than quality; and as a greater extent of soil was appropriated to these crops, so the area of slavery increased. The introduction of sugar-growing into Barbados, and the other West Indian Islands, was followed by an increase in the proportion of slaves to free inhabitants; and the acquisition of new territory in the United States caused a constant demand for a further extension of the slave system.

Slavery was suited to an aristocratic state of society; and indeed a community, where it exists, must necessarily be aristocratic: consequently the growth of a true democracy and of the modern democratic spirit was opposed to it. The importation of slaves was forced upon the democratic English colonies on the continent of America by the home government against their will; and, after the Declaration of Independence, it was resolved, that no more slaves should be imported into any of the thirteen United States. The Revolution in France was followed by emancipation in the French Colony of St. Domingo. The Spanish American republics abolished slavery, while the mother country, from which they revolted, continued to sanction it. If emancipation in the West Indies was finally forced on by the English government; it was because England had become more democratic and more progressive than her West Indian colonies. And if the slave system long held out in the Republic of the United States; it must be remembered that it survived only in the aristocratic Southern provinces, and that it was finally and forcibly put down by the Republicans of the North.

Similarly it has been the democratic religions which have most strongly opposed the institution of slavery, and the loudest protests against it have been those of Puritans and Quakers.

It has already been pointed out that it is difficult, consistently with historical accuracy, to brand any one race as being naturally more cruel than another. The nations of Europe have, one and all alike, to bear the reproach of having participated in the iniquity of slavery and the slave-trade. If the Portuguese, from being the first in the field on the West coast of Africa, were the originators of the traffic[1]; the Dutch are said to have imported the first cargo of slaves into the United States; and the English eventually claimed the monopoly of slave-trading, and worked it to the exclusion of other nations.

The laws relating to slavery were more inhuman and severe in the English and French than in the Spanish colonies[2]; and the Spanish planters in past times compared favourably with other Europeans in the treatment of their slaves. In later days, on the other hand, the Northern peoples of Europe claim the credit for the good work of abolishing the slave-trade and slavery of every description; the Danes, according to Heeren, having been the first to declare against the traffic in the case of their own dependencies[3]: and slavery now lingers only in the colonies of the Latin races, in the Spanish dependency of Cuba, and in the empire of Brazil.

Most people at the present day think of slavery, in civilised countries, as belonging to the distant past: but if we

[1] In 1620.   [2] See reference given in chap. vi.   [3] In 1792.

CHAPTER IV.

3rd class.
a. Convicts.

remember, that it has only within the memory of living man ceased to be an integral element in the social system of America and the West Indies; that it has not yet entirely died out in Cuba and Brazil; that it prevails throughout a great part of Asia, and the greatest part of Africa; and that it lingers still in Turkey and Egypt; it will be seen at once how deeply rooted has been the evil, how gradual has been its abolition, and how modern is the belief, that to buy and sell men and women is an iniquity in the sight of God and man.

10. The feeling against slavery is based on moral grounds. Slavery is now held by most civilised men to be absolutely wrong at all times and under all circumstances. But when we turn to consider the class of criminals and convicts, who have also played an important part in colonisation, the same reasoning does not apply. The objection to a system of transportation is relative to the conditions under which it is carried out. Bacon[1], it is true, lays down that "it is a shameful and unblessed thing to take the scum of people and wicked condemned men to be the people with whom you plant: and not only so but it spoileth the plantation: for they will ever live like rogues, and not fall to work, but be lazy and do mischief and spend victuals and be quickly weary, and then certify over to their country to the discredit of the plantation:" but it is clear that a statement of this kind is too general, and requires considerable modification. In itself, there is nothing immoral in disposing of criminals in one locality rather than in another. The question of right or wrong depends upon the particular circumstances of time and place. It must be wrong to ship men off, by way of punishment, however criminal, to a hopelessly unhealthy climate, such as Cayenne[2], where the French have established a penal

---

[1] 'Essay on Plantations.'
[2] The French have for more than twenty years, however, sent to Cayenne not European but coloured convicts from their colonial dependencies.

settlement. It is wrong to place them where they will infect the native inhabitants, or where there is a large population of honest settlers, who object to having their colony made the receptacle of the off-scourings of the mother country. And it is wrong again to place them where they will not be under proper control, or where their treatment cannot be scrutinised and checked by public opinion. As a matter of fact, one or other of these drawbacks must always exist; and hence the feeling of the time, at least in England, has become more and more opposed, and rightly so, to any system of transportation. But, in the abstract[1], there is something to be said for the theory, that the criminal outcast of civilised society is likely to develop some form of usefulness in less civilised surroundings. The ablest and most energetic of the Brazilians, the Paulistas, sprang in part from convict stock: and Darwin's judgment on the results of transportation to the Australian colonies deserves always to be borne in mind[2]. Writing of his visit to Tasmania, in 1836, he says, in an often quoted passage: "On the whole as a place of punishment the object is scarcely gained: as a real system of reform it has failed as perhaps would every other plan. But as a means of making men outwardly honest, of converting vagabonds most useless in one hemisphere into active citizens of another, and thus giving birth to a new and splendid country, a grand centre of civilisation, it has succeeded to a degree perhaps unparalleled in history." And if any regular system of transportation to English colonies can now no longer be defended, little can be said against the humanity of sending out child-criminals, under due precautions, not to undergo penal sentences abroad, but to try and start a new life away from their old and bad associations.

In treating of the subject of criminals as material for forming a colony, it must be remembered, in the first place,

---

[1] See Bordier, 'Colonisation Scientifique.'
[2] 'Voyage of the Beagle,' chap. xiii.

CHAPTER IV.

that it was not easy in old times to induce men to leave their homes and cross the seas, except for some pressing motive of poverty or crime. Accordingly prisoners were supplied to Frobisher and Cartier[1], by the English and French governments respectively, to enable them to carry on their exploring and colonising work in North America. And earlier still, in 1497[2], the Spanish government issued two edicts, one allowing judicial transportation of criminals to the West Indies, and the other giving indulgence to criminals, with certain exceptions, on condition of their going out to Hispaniola at their own expense, to serve for a specified time under Columbus.

It must be borne in mind too that the class which we are considering included in past times many besides the ordinary felon. Under this head must be placed colonists, whose only crime in the mother country was their poverty: such were the men whom Oglethorpe took out to Georgia from the debtors' prisons in England. The list comprises also religious and political offenders, whom the government of the day found it convenient to ship off beyond the seas. For instance, among the earliest colonists of Brazil were a number of Jews, whom the Portuguese government, in obedience to the calls of the Inquisition, transported together with a herd of common convicts. And English political malcontents were despatched, by Cromwell at one time, and James the Second at another, to the North American and West Indian colonies.

The Spanish edict, referred to above, authorised transportation as a punishment for crime; and the Portuguese marked out their Brazilian possessions to be a special receptacle for convicts. But England seems to have been the first country[3] to institute a definite and regular system of transporting convicted felons. And the record of the years,

---

[1] See Doyle's 'English in America,' vol. i. chap. iv. and v.
[2] See Helps' 'Conquest of America,' bk. ii. chap. ii.
[3] See Lewis, 'Government of Dependencies,' chap. vi.

during which the system was in force, shows that the merits of the question must, as has been already stated, be considered in relation to the particular conditions of time and place.

Convicts have from time to time been sent to various English dependencies, for instance to Gibraltar and Bermuda. And certain colonies, as Sierra Leone and the Cape, have been intended to receive penal settlements, (the project having been abandoned in the case of Sierra Leone owing to the unhealthiness of the climate, and in that of the Cape on account of the opposition of the colonists). But it is with Australia that the history of transportation has been mainly connected.

After the American colonies had declared their independence, it was determined to send convicts to Australia, partly because they could no longer be sent to the United States, and partly because it was considered necessary to ratify the English claim to the Australian continent by planting a colony on its shores. And as it was difficult to find men who were ready of their own free will to emigrate to a distant and practically unknown land, the government determined to provide the services of involuntary colonists.

The first batch of convicts was sent to New South Wales in 1787, the last consignment to Western Australia was despatched in 1867; and the history of the intervening period shows how rapidly and completely public opinion changed on the subject of transportation.

Opposition to the system sprang up in England, when the horrors due to the want of proper control and of separation became fully known. As one Australian colony after another became the home of a constantly increasing number of free settlers, the colonists themselves became more and more opposed to the introduction of criminals from outside. And the final death-blow was given to the system by the rush of immigrants, which followed on the discovery of gold in

Victoria in 1851. At the present time, the strength of the feeling in Australia against the results of transportation may be gauged by the recent outcry of the colonists, against the existence of a French penal settlement within measurable distance of the continent, and the loud expression of their fears, that the Australian shores may be contaminated by the landing of convicts or ex-convicts from New Caledonia.

In this latter island the French government are still trying the experiment, which the English have abandoned, and still hope to make respectable colonists out of the criminal population of the mother country. Australia has been taken as their model: and the stages have been carefully elaborated, by which the convict graduates into a free citizen; passing from prison to family life, to landed proprietorship, and to more and more unrestricted communion with the outer world. The theory is at once sound and attractive: but, in view of past experience, it may well be doubted whether the practical results of the system would bear detailed examination, or be found to be more satisfactory in New Caledonia than they have proved elsewhere.

b. Indentured coolies.

11. The last kind of colonist to be noticed is the class of indentured coolies. The system of emigration under contract to labour for a term of years is of no modern origin. Labourers were supplied in this way to the Virginian plantations in the early days of English colonisation [1]: and it was found necessary to make stringent provisions against the practice of kidnapping on the part of the labour contractors, who shipped off their victims from the port of Bristol; and to take legal steps, to prevent the indentured labourer from becoming a slave.

It was the abolition of slavery, however, which led to the present system. The sugar-growing colonies required a constant and steady supply of labour to replace the negro

---

[1] See Doyle's 'History of the English in America,' vol. i. chap. xiii.

slaves; and resort was had to the over-populated East to provide workmen for the West Indian plantations. Except to a small extent at first, the supply has not been drawn from Africa; but from other sources, which have been comparatively free from the taint of slavery, from China and British India. And latterly, as far at least as most of[1] the English colonies are concerned, the contract system has, mainly on grounds of expense, been confined to Indian coolies [2].

It would be out of place here to enter into the details of the system, which has been carefully organised by the English government, in order to preserve the freedom of their Indian subjects. It is clear that, without due supervision, there must always be a danger of the coolie traffic degenerating into a modified slave-trade, and of the labourer becoming more or less enslaved: and the danger is increased, by the difficulty of making members of a half civilised race understand the position in which they are placed by the terms of their contract, and the protection to which they are entitled from the law. The treatment recorded of Chinese coolies in the Guano islands of Peru, and the abuses which from time to time have been brought to light in connexion with the Pacific labour traffic, are evidence of the necessity, which is laid on any civilised government, of keeping coolie immigration strictly under control.

The essence of the contract system is to send immigrants to colonies for a term of years only, not to provide permanent settlers; and in most cases return passages

---

[1] Polynesians are, and were a few years ago to a much greater extent, imported into some of the Australasian colonies, especially Queensland, under a system of contract by indenture. The importation of these islanders is safeguarded by the Imperial Pacific Islanders Protection Acts.
[2] A full account of the system under which Indian coolies are imported into the colonies will be found in the Colonisation Circular for 1877, issued by the emigration board of the Colonial Office.

after a certain period of service form one condition of the contract: but the practical result of this form of immigration, in the West Indies, and still more in Mauritius, has been, that a large Indian element has been added to the permanent population, an element which grows in importance year by year: and in a few generations it may be found, that the importation of coolie labourers has in effect become a great measure of state-controlled colonisation.

CHAPTER V.

NATIONS WHICH HAVE COLONISED.

1. *Ancient.*

1. THE most conspicuous nations in the field of colonisation have been, in ancient times the Phoenicians, including the Carthaginian branch of the race, the Greeks, and the Romans: in modern ages, the Spaniards, the Portuguese, the Dutch, the French, and the English.

2. Civilisation has moved westward and seaward. Its history began on the great rivers, the Nile and the Euphrates; it gradually shifted its scenes to the shores of the Mediterranean, to Phoenicia, Greece and Rome, moving always from East to West; and so passed on as modern history to the open Atlantic. It is with the intermediate, the Mediterranean stage, that the colonies of the ancient world are connected. Those colonies were almost entirely confined to the coasts of the inland sea. It is true that the Phoenicians and Carthaginians penetrated far into the Atlantic; but their line of colonies stretched only a little way along the south-west shores of Spain, and the north-west shores of Africa; no Greek settlement was planted outside the Straits of Gibraltar; and all the early Roman colonies were within the limits of the Italian peninsula.

3. The history of the Mediterranean peoples is a history of cities, not of countries; and the colonies, which they founded, were essentially town communities. Rome alone grew out of a city into a country and an empire, just as she alone was great enough in her later history to pass beyond the basin of the Mediterranean, and to form provinces

CHAPTER V.

and plant settlements in the North and West of Europe. And yet, even in the days of Augustus or Trajan, the city of Rome was far more than merely the chief town of the Roman dominions: the English Empire is the Empire of England, not of London; the Roman Empire, on the other hand, was from first to last the Empire, not of Italy, but of Rome. And as the states of the Mediterranean were mainly cities or confederations of cities; and their colonies, towns with no large extent of country attached to them: so in old days the term Colony[1] implied the people who emigrated, rather than, as in modern times, the territory colonised. And when we speak of Paris as the metropolis of France, or of Vienna as the metropolis of Austria, we forget that the true etymological meaning of the word 'metropolis' is not the chief town of a country or empire, but the mother city, the parent of separate city states.

The fact of the population being collected in towns, instead of being spread uniformly over a large tract of country, gave a powerful impulse to colonisation. Numbers soon pressed upon the limited space, and social and political quarrels were embittered by the difficulty which people found in getting out of each other's way: hence the στάσεις, or party feuds, of the Greek and Phoenician cities led to a large amount of emigration.

The Phoenicians.

4. The Phoenicians[2], however, were a far more commercial race than either the Greeks or the Romans: if some of their colonies were due to dissensions at home and to consequent emigration, the greater number were planted by the state as trading depôts on islands or on the coasts of the mainland. And, being more commercial than the Greeks, they went further afield; they sent their colonists from the extreme East to the extreme West of the Mediterranean, and even

---

[1] Lewis, 'Government of Dependencies,' chap. iii.
[2] For what is said of the Phoenicians and Carthaginians see Heeren, Asiatic and African Nations,' and Lewis, 'Government of Dependencies.'

passed into the outer ocean. They traded with the Iberians and monopolised the treasures of the Andalusian mines. They planted their great colony of Cadiz beyond the Straits of Gibraltar. Advancing northwards step by step, they reached at last the Scilly Isles and the tin-diggings on the mainland of Cornwall. They or their Carthaginian descendants, perhaps both the one and the other, sent their ships to Madeira. They sailed round Africa; and, in the East, they appear to have established trading stations in the Arabian Sea and the Persian Gulf.

The chief object of their commerce was mineral, especially gold, silver and tin. Similarly the precious metals were the chief object of Spanish merchants and explorers at the outset of modern history: and the mines of Spain were to the Phoenicians what the American mines were, in after ages, to the men who followed Columbus.

Before 700 B.C. the merchant sailors of Tyre and Sidon were, to quote Grote's words[1], 'the exclusive navigators of the Mediterranean.' They colonised Cyprus, Crete, Rhodes, Thasos, and other islands of the Aegean, and planted settlements on the coasts of the Black Sea and the Propontis. But they were gradually driven out of the Aegean and the eastern part of the Mediterranean by the Greeks, except in Cyprus, at the threshold of their own country, where, as in Sicily, the two rival nations continued side by side; and, in historical times, their colonies were to be found on the north coast of Africa, stretching westward from the territory of the Greek settlement of Cyrene, in Sicily, in Malta, in Sardinia, in the Balearic Isles, and in Spain. In Gaul and Italy they found no footing, but left these countries to their own inhabitants and to the Greek immigrants; adopting as their main principle of trade and colonisation, either to be exclusive masters of the situation or not to intrude at all.

4. The greatest of the Phoenician colonies was Carthage, *The Carthaginian.*

[1] History of Greece, chap. xviii.

50   GEOGRAPHY OF THE COLONIES.

CHAPTER V.

which owed its foundation to the disputes of political factions in the mother city Tyre : and Carthage in her turn became a coloniser on a large scale, and a ruler to an extent unknown to any of the other Phoenician towns. The Phoenicians, like the Greeks, kept little or no control over their colonies : the Carthaginians, on the contrary, held their settlements and dependencies well in hand. This result was due in great measure to the geographical position of Carthage : she was more centrally placed with regard to her dependencies than were the mother cities of Phoenicia, and therefore had them, more within call. In ancient times, when communication was tedious and uncertain, it was difficult to keep a distant colony in a position of dependence; and it is worth noticing, that the two Mediterranean states which enjoyed the most central position, namely Carthage and Rome, were the most successful in holding together a foreign and colonial empire.

Historians distinguish two periods in Carthaginian history. During the first period Carthage was the rival of Greece; during the second she was the rival of Rome. The first began in the sixth century B.C., and lasted down to about the beginning of the first Punic war in the year 264 B.C. The second includes the years of the Punic wars, down to the final taking and destruction of the city in 146 B.C. Carthage became great as a commercial and a colonising state in the age preceding her long struggle with Rome. She gradually absorbed most of the old Phoenician settlements in the west of the Mediterranean (although some of the sister colonies, such as her near neighbour Utica, retained their independence), she became mistress of the western, the Phoenician, half of the north African coast. She gained a firm footing in Spain, and possessed herself of the Balearic Isles, Sardinia, Corsica, and the west of Sicily : and in addition she carried a chain of trading stations to the south-west along the coast of Morocco.

After the first Punic war, however, she entered upon a

different phase. Driven out of Sicily and Sardinia she tried to compensate herself by building up a Spanish empire. While in former times she had confined her efforts to maintaining trading settlements on the shores of the peninsula, and keeping up friendly commercial relations with the inland peoples, she now put on a more imperial dress, assumed a direct dominion over Spain as far as the line of the Ebro, and, under Hasdrubal's guidance, founded new Carthage to be the capital of Carthaginian Spain.

CHAPTER V.

Her new greatness however was shortlived. In less than forty years her power was broken: and successful as she had been while yet a maritime and commercial state, she proved no match for Rome in the work of building up an inland empire.

5. Carthage planted two kinds of colonies. The first were inland agricultural colonies in the territory of the subject Africans. They were similar to the Athenian κληρουχίαι, and to the Roman coloniae: they served the double purpose of holding down the native races, and providing lands for the poorer Carthaginian citizens. The second were commercial stations, intended to tap the trade of the different countries on the shores of which they were placed, and strictly confined to the original object of their foundation, that of being feeders to the imperial city.

Two classes of Carthaginian colonies.

As compared with the Greeks, the Carthaginians had some idea of keeping together a series of colonies and dependencies, and of forming a dominion: and, being practical men of business, they knew in their best days where to stop, and were not carried away by vague lust of conquest. But as compared with the Romans they failed to grow out of a city into an empire, and from first to last they followed an exclusive and oppressive policy to their subjects and colonists.

Some parallel to them may be found in the Venetians in the Middle Ages; and later in the Dutch, to whom[1] Heeren compares them in their mode of colonisation. Venice, like

Comparison of Carthaginians with Venetians and Dutch.

[1] 'African Nations,' p. 24.

CHAPTER V.

The Greeks. Two classes of Greek colonies. (1) The ἀποικίαι or Greek colonies proper.

Carthage, was a maritime commercial city-state, governed by a merchant oligarchy, fighting her battles with mercenary troops, a harsh monopolist in her relations with her dependencies[1], and utilising her colonies for the purpose of enriching her poorer citizens. Like the Carthaginians, the Dutch have been an almost purely commercial race; and their settlements have been trading settlements, planted mainly on islands. They too have pursued a policy of rigid monopoly in regard to the trade of their colonies, and their history shows that Holland never expanded into a Dutch empire. She remained, and still remains, a small European state, with a long train of foreign possessions, which have always been regarded as tributaries to, rather than as one with, the mother country.

The Greeks, though a trading and maritime race, were not so exclusively commercial as the Phoenicians. The Greek colonies proper, the ἀποικίαι, were very far from being mere trading stations. They originated, as has been seen, in over-population, or in social or political quarrels; the story of the foundation of Cyrene by emigrants from the island of Thera being a good instance of the manner in which economical distress, political discontent, and social inequalities, combined to promote Greek colonisation. They were as a rule not planted by the government of the mother city; and, in their relations to it, they were 'somewhat similar to the English colonies in America, especially after the independence of the latter[2].' From the first they were separate towns, the citizens of which represented the surplus population of certain other towns.

Like the Phoenicians and Carthaginians, the Greeks settled on islands and sea-coasts, and did not, at any rate till the time of the Macedonians, make any attempt to acquire any large continental dominions. Greek life was town life

---

[1] See 'Government of Dependencies,' chap. ii.
[2] 'Government of Dependencies,' chap. ii; but contrast Niebuhr, 'Lectures on Ancient History,' Lecture xxix.

carried to an extreme, and no pure Greek state rose beyond the limit of being the chief city in a confederation.

All the eastern coasts of the Mediterranean, with the exception of Phoenicia, were colonised by the Greeks. The islands of the Aegean passed into their hands, and even in Phoenician Cyprus they founded a Salamis. A series of Hellenic settlements encircled the Black Sea and the Sea of Marmora. Greek colonists planted themselves in the Crimean peninsula, and placed Byzantium to command for ever the passage of the Bosphorus. The Athenian Miltiades, the victor of Marathon, reigned in the Thracian Chersonnese; and the Greek cities in and near Chalcidice, Potidaea, Olynthus, Therme and others, played an important part both in earlier and later Greek history. Corinth sent settlers northwards along the coast of the Adriatic to Corcyra and Epidamnus. In Italy, Cumae, like many later Greek cities the colony of a colony, was planted far back in prehistoric times upon the Campanian shores; and the southern peninsula, containing the great cities of Sybaris, Croton, Locri, Tarentum, and many others, became so completely Hellenised, as to be known under the name of Magna Graecia. In Sicily such towns as Syracuse and Agrigentum were great enough to hold their own against the Carthaginian power. In the south of France, the enterprising Phocaeans, who had already planted the unsuccessful colony of Alalia in Corsica, founded the seaport of Massalia; which held a position in ancient days little if at all inferior in relative importance to the modern Marseilles. And the Massalians, in their turn, inheriting the boldness of their ancestors, trespassed upon the Phoenician preserves, and planted five settlements on the east coast of Spain. Lastly, on the north shores of Africa, between the borders of Egypt and the Carthaginian frontier, in what is now the province of Tripoli, the Dorians found a site for settlements of their race, the greatest and best-known of which was the city of Cyrene.

CHAPTER V.

It is noteworthy, that the Greek colonies in most instances became great before the cities of Greece proper. Miletus, whose origin was traced back directly to the prytaneum of Athens, became the most powerful of the Ionic towns in Asia Minor, sent out colonies in her turn to the Black Sea and the coasts of Thrace, and fell under the sway first of the Lydians and subsequently of the Persians, before Athens had shown any signs of greatness. Tarentum, the child of Sparta, soon outstripped the mother village. And the Corinthian colony of Syracuse grew out of all comparison with Corinth herself.

As Adam Smith points out[1], the colonists found more land and more room for expansion in their new homes than in the mother cities: and something must be attributed to the readiness with which the Greeks[2], especially the members of the Ionic branch, assimilated themselves to and intermarried with the native races, making friends of their neighbours; adding to their own population; and rejecting in the colonies much of the exclusiveness, which characterised and confined the citizens of the older Greek communities.

(2) *The Athenian κληρουχίαι.*

The Athenian κληρουχίαι, to which allusion has been made, were of a totally different character from the ordinary Greek colonies. They were similar to the agricultural settlements planted by Carthage in Libya, and also to the Roman coloniae, though without having so distinctly a military character as most of the latter[3]. They consisted of allotments of land, in the territory not of barbarian tribes but of conquered Greeks, made by the Athenian government to Athenian citizens; and they were employed at once to punish and hold in check the conquered state, and to provide for the conquerors. Land was thus appropriated in Aegina, in Euboea, in many of the Aegean islands, in Thrace, and in the

---

[1] Chapter on Causes of Prosperity in New Colonies.
[2] See Curtius, 'History of Greece,' bk. ii. chap. iii.
[3] See 'Government of Dependencies,' chap. ii.

Chersonnese. How widely these cleruchies differed from the ἀποικίαι, or Greek colonies proper[1], is shown by the fact, that in some cases, as in that of Mitylene, the allottees of the land either never emigrated at all, or returned after a while to Athens, playing the part of absentee landlords and drawing rents from the old owners of the soil. This system of colonisation was peculiar to Athens, the greatest of the Greek states; and is one of the few indications of an imperial policy, which are to be found in the history of Greece. It attained its fullest development during the administration of Pericles, the greatest statesman whom Greece produced, and one of the very few Greeks who seem to have conceived the idea of a Greek empire and a Greek nation, as opposed to a mere collection of small rival municipalities.

In the main, Greek colonisation, like Greek history and Greek geography, was disjointed. Enterprising, commercial, at home on the sea, self-reliant, and ready to adapt themselves to any circumstances, the Greeks could emigrate and found colonies. But they had no cohesion and no power of ruling; they could not grow out of municipal into imperial ways; and so no Greek state can be said to have made or held a colonial empire.

6. Unlike the Greeks and Phoenicians, the Romans were not a maritime race. The 'ambition of the Romans,' says Gibbon[2], 'was confined to the land; nor was that warlike people ever actuated by the enterprising spirit, which had prompted the navigators of Tyre, of Carthage, and even of Marseilles, to enlarge the bounds of the world and to explore the most remote coasts of the ocean.' They were not, again, to any great extent a commercial race; nor had they the power of assimilation which was possessed by the Greeks. They were an agricultural and military people, gradually enlarging the borders of their territory by force of arms,

The Romans.

---

[1] See Boeckh, 'Public Economy of Athens.'
[2] Chapter i.

CHAPTER V.

and developing, as none of the other Mediterranean states developed, into a continental power.

The Phoenicians and Greeks extended their range by planting settlements, which had little geographical or political connexion with Phoenicia or Greece. The expansion of the Carthaginians and Romans on the contrary, holding, as has been shown, a more central position, was geographically continuous. Rome was the centre of a circle with an ever widening circumference. She consolidated Southern Italy, took in Sicily, Sardinia, Corsica, and the land between the Po and the Alps. She constituted herself the heir of the Carthaginians and the Greeks, and gradually extended her dominion north and south, east and west. When the empire attained its widest dimensions under Trajan, it included not only all the Mediterranean lands, but practically the whole of the world as then known. All Western Europe up to the Rhine was under Roman dominion, and Britain was a subject province. The line of the Danube had been passed, and the province of Dacia constituted in what is now Roumanian and Hungarian territory. In the East the empire touched the Caspian and the Persian Gulf; its frontiers stretched far down the Red Sea on both the Arabian and Egyptian sides; and the whole of the northern coast of Africa belonged to Rome.

The Romans were not merely a fighting race, they were also a race of rulers. When they had made a conquest, and acquired a dependency, they knew how to retain it. Their legacies to the world have been the law, which they formulated and administered, and the roads, radiating out from Rome to all quarters of the world, by which they overcame the difficulties of communication, and kept their provinces together.

They held their dependencies partly by their garrisons, partly by their policy and good government: for when compared not only with other ancient peoples, but also with the nations of Western Europe down to very recent times, it must be allowed that they governed well. Law was enforced; justice was in the main dealt out between man and man; and if many of their pro-consuls were oppressive and unjust, the history of the colonies and dependencies of modern Europe will furnish instances of equally great injustice and oppression. The iniquities of Verres in Sicily are paralleled by the cruelty and rapacity of the Portuguese governors who succeeded Albuquerque in India: and if Romans of the type of Sallust amassed vast fortunes in the provinces, they were no worse than the English Nabobs of the time of Clive, who left England for India penniless men, and after a course of years returned home millionaires.

Further the policy of the Romans broadened with the growth of their empire. Imperial took the place of municipal views, the franchise was extended, and the Roman citizenship was given first to the Italians, subsequently to the provincials. While, as a sovereign race, they kept a strong hand on their dependencies, they yet allowed some amount of Home Rule; and whether dealing with Greeks or Jews or Egyptians, they ordinarily interfered but little with local customs and creeds. The consequence of combining military strength with good administration and liberal statesmanship was that, instead of losing their dependencies one by one at the first sign of pressure from without, as was the case with other ancient states, they held together an enormous empire for generation after generation.

The Roman coloniae[1], as the term implies, bore the character of agricultural settlements. No colonist was sent out from Rome without receiving a prescribed quantity of land in his new home. Colonisation in the sense of unauthorised voluntary emigration to uninhabited or savage lands had no place in the Roman system. The colonies, like the cleruchies, were purely the work of the state: they were allotments of land in conquered territory, made by the

[1] See chap. i. on meaning of 'colonia.'

CHAPTER V.

Four stages of coloniae,

(1) The Coloniae civium Romanorum.

(2) The Latin colonies.

(3) The Gracchan colonies.

(4) The later Roman colonies.

government, with a view at once to holding the subject peoples in check and to providing land for the poorer citizens of Rome.

The different kinds of Roman colonies, and the various rights which each kind enjoyed, have been more debated than almost any other subject in ancient history, and the question is too complicated to be here discussed. The early colonies appear to have been planted simply as outposts of the Roman race among the subject Latins and Italians. The earliest of all, the coloniae civium Romanorum, were garrisons of Roman citizens placed in the conquered towns, and endowed with land at the expense of the inhabitants of those towns. These colonies were succeeded by the Latin colonies. Under this latter system the incoming Romans were merged in the Latin or Italian community; and the whole was constituted a colonia and became a part of the Roman state, though without enjoying the full privileges of Roman citizenship. At the time of the Gracchi a new set of colonies came into existence: they were intimately connected with the agrarian laws, and with the proposed resumption by the government of the state domains. They were designed as a democratic measure to relieve the distress which existed among the poorer citizens of Rome, and to draw off the surplus population of the city. With their introduction the area of Roman colonisation was widened, one of the new settlements, planted by Caius Gracchus on the site where Carthage had stood, being the first transmarine colony of Rome.

The latest phase of Roman colonisation, like the earliest, took the form of military settlement. Sulla provided for 120,000 of his soldiers by allotments of land throughout Italy; and, under the empire, the provinces were studded, especially on the frontiers of the north and west, with coloniae composed of retired soldiers, who were paid by land grants for doing garrison duty.

CHAPTER V.

Twenty-five colonies of this kind are said to have been planted in Spain, and nine in Britain[1]; and the name of Lincoln like that of Cologne still recalls the generic term Colonia.

Modern colonisation implies maritime enterprise, commercial activity, exploration of unknown lands, and the creation of new settlements in a virgin soil: all this was unknown to the Romans. Like the Russians at the present day they gradually conquered their neighbours, and retained their conquests by an unbroken chain of communications. They were military despots, but they gave to their dependencies equality in subjection: they enforced order and maintained the law: and they stand out to all times as a conspicuous example of a governing race.

[1] Gibbon, chap. ii. note 32.

CHAPTER VI.

NATIONS WHICH HAVE COLONISED.

2. *Modern.*

CHAPTER VI.

Beginnings of modern colonisation.

1. IN the Middle Ages, though the element of discovery was wanting, Genoa and Venice proved that colonising commercial city-states were still to be found in the Mediterranean. But, with the finding of America, as Prof. Seeley lately pointed out in 'The Expansion of England[1],' the centre of European civilisation gradually shifted from the south to the west, from the inland sea to the outer ocean; and a new and broader field was opened for the formation of colonies. Yet the Mediterranean may claim to have been the birthplace of the new order of things. Genoa gave Columbus to Spain, Venice gave the Cabots[2] to England.

The Spaniards and Portuguese.

2. The earliest of the colonising nations in modern Europe were the two Latin peoples, the Spaniards and Portuguese. This was the natural consequence of their geographical position between the Mediterranean and the Atlantic. The Spaniards went chiefly to the West, the Portuguese chiefly to the East, and a Papal bull issued in 1493 drew a line between them. But, notwithstanding, the best specimen of Portuguese colonisation is to be found in Brazil: and the largest and most populous of the remaining Spanish dependencies are the Philippines in the East Indies.

Of the two nations, the Portuguese were the first in the field, gradually working their way down the west coast of Africa. But Columbus discovered America for Spain some five years

---

[1] Lecture V.
[2] As to the question whether the Cabots were Genoese or Venetian, see Appendix C to Doyle's 'History of the English in America,' vol. i.

PACIFIC OCEAN
WORLD
on Mercator's Projection
by Keith Johnston F.R.S.E.

Showing Spanish & Portuguese Colonizations.
Spanish Colonies now lost to Spain Coloured
Present Spanish Colonies
Portuguese Colonies now lost to Portugal
Present Portuguese Colonies

before Vasco da Gama led his countrymen to India round the Cape of Good Hope; and the rapidity, with which Spanish exploration and conquest spread over a vast area, gives them some claim to be placed first in the list of the colonising peoples of modern history.

CHAPTER VI.

3. Reference has been already made in previous chapters to the Spanish race and character, and to the circumstances under which Spain became a colonising power. A mixed race themselves[1], the Spaniards were ready to intermingle with the races with whom they were brought into contact. A fighting, ruthless, and fanatical people, having vanquished the heathen at home, they were prepared to carry their conquests into other lands. At the end of the fifteenth century, the spirit of adventure, the desire of gold, and the crusading impulse all combined to stimulate and influence the Spanish mind: and the strong and ambitious government of Spain was only too ready to sanction schemes of annexation and conquest, hoping by such means to increase the prestige of the country, to add to its material resources, and so to make it the leading power of the world.

Spanish colonisation.

4. Spanish colonisation began on islands. The Canaries are the oldest Spanish colony[2], having been acquired in the middle of the fifteenth century; while the settlement in the island of Hispaniola or Hayti was the first result of the voyages of Columbus. And the dependencies which are now left to Spain consist almost entirely of islands, as the Philippines in the East, Cuba and Porto Rico in the West Indies.

Extent and nature of Spanish colonial empire.

But though it began with islands and is ending with islands, the Spanish colonial empire was in its great days essentially a

---

[1] This is pointed out by Raynal in 'The East and West Indies,' bk. viii. See also Bordier, 'Colonisation Scientifique,' chap. iv.

[2] For the early history of the Canaries, see the beginning of Helps' 'Spanish Conquest of America,' and the 'Conquest of the Canaries' in the Hakluyt series. They were finally secured to Castile by treaty with Portugal in 1479.

CHAPTER VI.

continental empire. Starting from the West Indies, all of which were claimed by Spain, though the smaller islands were left to be appropriated by foreign interlopers, the Spaniards invaded the mainland. They extended their sway over the whole of Central and South America, with the exception of Guiana and Brazil; on the west, from San Francisco in California to the river Biobio in Chili; on the east from St. Augustine in the north of Florida to the mouth of the La Plata river, and nominally even to the Straits of Magellan. As the Western world had been assigned to Spain by the Pope, she wisely interfered little in the East. Her dependency of the Philippines was regarded, and rightly regarded, as an extension of the Spanish empire in the West. It was annexed to America, not to Europe. The Philippines were discovered by Magellan on his voyage round the world in 1521, a voyage which was designed with a view to discovering a western route to the Spice Islands; the first Spanish settlement in them was formed in 1565; and the year 1571 saw the foundation of Manilla. Near the Philippines is the Sulu archipelago; and the straight route from Central America to Manilla lies through the Caroline and the Mariannes or Ladrones Islands. Over these groups Spanish sovereignty or Spanish claims extend, but otherwise the colonising and conquering power of Spain has been confined to the Western hemisphere.

Defects of Spanish colonisation.

5. Her vast American dominions were the result of rapid conquest, not of gradually growing commercial settlement. In North America, the English made slow way in a desolate land, among scattered savage tribes which could be exterminated but not enslaved[1]. The course of the Spaniards was widely different. In Mexico and Peru, they conquered at a blow nations which were rich, powerful, and well organised; but which had long been broken in to despotism, and when once subdued became the slaves of the conquerors. The conquest of Mexico was effected in less than three

---

[1] See Doyle, 'English in America,' vol. i. chap. v.

NATIONS WHICH HAVE COLONISED.—MODERN. 63

years, that of Peru in some ten or eleven years, and nearly the whole of the Spanish possessions in America were acquired within sixty years from the date when Columbus first set sail from Spain. English colonisation in North America was from the first colonisation in its true sense [1]. It consisted of settlements in which there was no native element to be found: and in spite of isolated instances of intermingling, such as are pourtrayed in the romantic story of Pocahuntas, the English and the Indians lived entirely outside each other [2]. The Spanish American colonies, on the other hand, were simply conquered dependencies, containing a large native population. The Spanish conquest was too rapid to produce sound and beneficial results: the conquerors lost their heads, plunged into cruelty and extravagance, glutted themselves with gold and silver instead of quietly developing commerce and agriculture; and, yielding to the temptations of their position and the enervating influence of climate, in no long time degenerated in mind and body. The home government might have checked the pace at which the work was carried on: but if well-meaning it was unwise; it constantly sanctioned fresh conquests, and encouraged [3] the colonisation of the mainland before the colonies on the islands were well and healthily established.

Allusion has been made to the greater tendency to state interference which exists, and always has existed, among Spaniards and French than among English. On the other hand, it must be remembered, that the Spanish settlements and conquests in America [4] were due, in the first instance, not to the direct action of the state, but to the enterprise of individual adventurers, as Columbus, Cortez and Pizarro. Yet even these adventurers were as a rule

CHAPTER VI.

---

[1] See Seeley, 'Expansion of England,' Lecture iii.
[2] See Prescott, 'Conquest of Peru,' bk. iii. chap. vii.
[3] See Helps, 'Spanish Conquest of America,' vol. i. bk. viii. chap. ii.
[4] See Adam Smith, 'Wealth of Nations,' chapter on Causes of Prosperity of New Colonies.

backed by government to a greater degree than early English explorers. Columbus received from the Spanish authorities two ships and the necessary funds for his first voyage; while Cabot received only the royal authority to sail from Bristol at his own expense, and that amount of favour was conditional on his paying a fifth of his net profits to the Crown [1].

The English government indeed up to the end of the sixteenth century had good reason to be chary of encouraging foreign enterprise. The resources of the country were scanty, and its power slight, as compared with the strength of Spain; and foreign enterprise meant in great measure trespassing on the preserves of other European nations, and collision with the powers which had been beforehand at the start and held or claimed to hold the field. So, while the Spanish sovereigns had no reason for discouraging adventure, except so far as the interest or the caprice of the moment or higher motives of humanity dictated, Elizabeth could only countenance Sir Francis Drake at the risk of involving her country in war.

When the first wave of Spanish conquest had spent itself, the interference of the home government with the colonies became more and more pronounced. The Spanish rulers, like the Spanish adventurers, looked to America for a direct return of gold and silver, more than for any revenue from indirect sources. They regarded their new possessions simply as producing so much tribute, and hence they watched them very closely and kept them strictly under control. The results of this policy were fatal to the satisfactory development of the American dependencies of Spain. The elements of decay in the mother country were carefully imported into America; the political despotism, the undue power of the Church, and the social and commercial exclusiveness. 'The vices of the feudal government,' says Humboldt, writing

[1] See Doyle, 'English in America,' vol. i. chap. iv.

at the beginning of the present century, 'have passed from the one hemisphere to the other[1].' Political freedom was not to be found in Spain, the land which produced and put up with Philip II; much less could it exist in her subject dependencies.

The Roman Catholic Church, which had done so much to crush out any independence of mind at home, flourished in full force with rich endowments, pomp, and ceremonial, throughout the length and breadth of Spanish America: and even where the Jesuit missions did real work among the natives, the keystone of the system was absolute obedience to the Church. The social distinctions between races and classes were carefully maintained. The official appointments were all held by natives of Spain, creoles being jealously excluded. The land was tied up by strict entails or 'mayorazgos' as they were termed; so that Humboldt wrote, 'the property of new Spain, like that of old Spain, is in a great measure in the hands of a few powerful families who have gradually absorbed the smaller estates[2].' Lastly, the system of commercial monopoly was carried to a greater extreme by Spain than by any other country of Europe; all foreigners being excluded from the Spanish Indies[3], and the trade with the colonies being, until the middle of the eighteenth century, confined to a certain number of ships each year, and to the single port first of Seville, and subsequently of Cadiz.

6. At the same time there was a good side to the colonial policy of Spain: the influence and power of the State were time after time, from the reign of Isabella onwards, used to check, by laws and regulations and the appointment of Protectors of Indians, the cruelties which the natives suffered

Good points in the colonial policy of Spain.

---

[1] 'Political Essay on New Spain,' chap. x.
[2] See Humboldt as *sup.* See also Adam Smith, 'Wealth of Nations,' Chapter on Causes of Prosperity of New Colonies; and Raynal, 'History of European Settlements and Trade in East and West Indies,' book viii.
[3] See Raynal, book viii.

CHAPTER VI.

at the hands of private adventurers; and here as elsewhere it was to be seen that the safeguard of the native races in a conquered dependency is to be found in the home government. The legal protection given to the negro slaves in the Spanish Colonies, and the recognition of clearly defined rights in their case, testified to the advantage which may come from state interference[1]. And lastly it must be noted to the praise of the Spanish government, that they took the lead in establishing some definite system for the management of their Colonial Empire; the Council of the Indies being 'the earliest attempt to exercise constantly a vigilant control over the subordinate governments of dependencies by means of a separate public department in the dominant country[2].' Spain held her Colonial Empire for some three centuries, from 1500 to 1800: during the greater part of this period she was in a hopelessly weak, decayed, and corrupt condition, and it is impossible to suppose that she would have been able nevertheless to retain so long a vast continental dominion at a great distance from home, but for the advantage of having been from the first systematic in her dealings with the Colonies.

General results.

7. The history of Spain is the history of a power which rose quickly to a great height and then as quickly declined. The Spaniards were a fighting and conquering race, but they were not traders to any great extent, and they did not, in spite of redeeming points, succeed as governors. There was an absence among them of steady progress and development. There was no growth of liberty, no tendency to equality, no gradual expansion of view on the part of either the government or the nation. They regarded their colonies as tributaries to the mother country: they did not train them to

---

[1] See Humboldt, 'Narrative of Travels in Equinoctial Regions of America.' He gives the four rights of slaves under Spanish law, and compares their position in the different European colonies. See also Merivale, 'Colonisation and the Colonies.'

[2] 'Government of Dependencies,' chap. ii.

self-government: they lost them as suddenly as they gained them, and left them to be, as they are at the present day, a set of restless, unstable, and ill-organised communities.

Portuguese colonisation.

8. Inspired and trained by Prince Henry the Navigator, the Portuguese began to explore the coast of Africa in the earlier part of the fifteenth century. Born in 1394, almost exactly a century before his countrymen finally opened up the passage to India round the Cape of Good Hope, Prince Henry was in the fullest sense the father of modern discovery and colonisation. The son of a Portuguese king and an English princess (Philippa, daughter of John of Gaunt), he seemed to combine in his nature the chivalrous daring of the Portuguese breed with the dogged perseverance of the English. His high position gave authority to schemes which would have been at once rejected if put forward by one of lower station. In war he had shown himself to be personally the bravest of the brave: his character was pure and unstained: and in devoting his life to the furtherance of exploration and discovery, he set himself patiently to temper the dreams of enthusiasm by the dry light of science. He stationed himself, and built his observatory, at Sagres on the extreme south-western promontory of Europe; and from thence he looked out to the Atlantic and the shores of Africa, as Moses looked from Pisgah to the Promised Land. He saw his vessels come and go, slowly but surely pressing southwards: but like Moses he did not live to see the full realisation of his hopes, for more than thirty years passed from the date of his death in 1460 before Vasco de Gama landed in the East.

Prince Henry the Navigator.

9. The dominion of Portugal out of Europe was, in Professor Freeman's words[1], 'not actually continuous with her own European territory, but it began near to it, and it was a natural consequence and extension of her European advance. The Asiatic and American dominion of Portugal grew out of

Expansion of Portugal.

---

[1] 'Historical Geography of Europe,' chap. xii. sect. iii.

CHAPTER VI.

Extent and nature of Portuguese colonial empire.

her African dominion, and her African dominion was the continuation of her growth in her own peninsula.'

Before the last decade of the century was reached[1], Portuguese sailors had found their way to Madeira, the Azores, and the Cape de Verde Islands, all of which still belong to Portugal: they had explored the Gambia; had planted on the Gold Coast the fort of Elmina, which still bears its old name; and had entered into friendly relations with the King of the Congo territory.

A notable advance was made in 1486, when Bartholomew Diaz rounded what he called the Stormy Cape, but what his more far-seeing sovereign renamed the Cape of Good Hope, and landed at Algoa Bay. But the brilliant period of Portuguese history may better be dated from the year 1498, when Vasco de Gama, profiting by his predecessor's experience, again rounded the Cape, crossed the Eastern ocean, and set foot on Indian soil at Calicut.

The East.

The great Portuguese empire in the East was built up within a very few years[2]. Albuquerque, the far-seeing, high-minded commander, to whose genius its greatness was mainly due, and who established the seat of government in the Island of Goa, died as early as 1515. During the 16th century the Portuguese power extended over the West and East coasts of Africa; the provinces of Angola on the West, and Mozambique on the East having been retained by Portugal down to the present day. One Admiral, De Nova, discovered the islands of Ascension and St. Helena. The pilot Tristan d'Acunha, discovered the islands in the South Atlantic which are still called after him, and also the great island of Madagascar. Mascarenhas discovered Bourbon in 1505, and gave his name to the island; the same name being

---

[1] For an account of early Portuguese exploration, see the 1st book of Helps' 'Spanish Conquest of America.'
[2] For a *résumé* of the Portuguese conquests in the East, see Birdwood, 'Report on the India Office Records.'

afterwards extended also to the sister islands of Mauritius and Rodriguez. The trade of the Red Sea was commanded by the possession of Aden and Socotra: that of the Persian Gulf was secured by subjecting the Bahrein islands, where the Phoenicians had in old times planted a trading station, and by taking Muscat in Arabia, and the Persian Island of Ormuz. The whole of the shores of India were practically in Portuguese hands. Their stations were to be found on the Indus, down the Western coast, where they still hold Diu Damas and Goa, up the Eastern or Coromandel side, and even in Bengal. They visited the Maldives; planted themselves in Ceylon, at Colombo, Jaffua, Galle and elsewhere; placed factories on the Burmese coast; formed a settlement at Malacca; and established a trade with Cochin China. In the East Indian Archipelago they held various possessions, including the Banda islands and the Moluccas (the Spanish claim to which was finally relinquished by Charles the Fifth in the year 1529 in consideration of a loan from the Portuguese government), and they still hold part of Timor. They visited Sumatra, though they had no possessions either in that island or Java. They discovered Borneo, the Celebes, New Guinea and Australia[1]. And finally they opened a trade with China and Japan, consolidating it by the possession of the island of Formosa[2], and of the station of Macao on the coast of China, which was ceded to them as late as 1586.

The history of Portuguese colonisation is mainly connected with the East; but their soundest work, as has been said, was done in Brazil, which was discovered in January 1500 by the Spaniard Pinzon, and three months later by the Portuguese Cabral. They conquered and formed great dependencies

Brazil.

---

[1] See Major, 'Life of Prince Henry of Portugal,' and what is said at p. 75 of this chapter with regard to Dutch discoveries.
[2] The Dutch however were the first European nation to form a settlement in Formosa, at Taiwan: see the interesting 'Sketch of Formosa,' lately published at Hongkong, by Messrs. Colquhoun and Lockhart.

CHAPTER VI.

among the nations of the East Indies; but in Brazil, inhabited only by savage tribes, they planted settlements of more permanent strength. Adam Smith's account of Brazil in his day is that 'no one colony in America is supposed to contain so great a number of people of European extraction[1].' And while in no long time the Portuguese power in the East broke down hopelessly before the Dutch, in Brazil the colony, to the founding of which government contributed little but involuntary settlers, showed such vigour and vitality, that the Dutch invaders were eventually obliged to leave the country and abandon their schemes of annexation.

The place held by Brazil in the Portuguese Empire may be compared to that which the Philippines filled in the Empire of Spain. As the latter islands were annexed from the West, and were in a sense a continuation of the Spanish American dominion, so Brazil was first discovered by a Portuguese fleet intended for the East, but carried out of its course by the winds of the Atlantic: and throughout its history it was intimately connected with the Portuguese possessions on the West Coast of Africa.

For years after Magellan had discovered the Philippines, the Spanish Government paid no attention to them, yet they subsequently became one of the most prosperous and satisfactory of the possessions of Spain. Similarly Brazil was, for some fifty years after Cabral's first visit to its shores, considered of little importance by the Portuguese authorities, because no precious metal was found in it: but in spite of the neglect— perhaps, as Adam Smith thought, on account of it[2]—'in time it grew up to be a great and powerful colony,' far surpassing in strength and solidity all the other colonies or dependencies of Portugal.

The Portuguese compared with the Spaniards.

10. Like the Spaniards, the Portuguese were a conquering and crusading race: they too had been trained in wars with

[1] Chapter on Causes of Prosperity of New Colonies.
[2] Ibid.

the Moors, from whom in 1415 Prince Henry, the great originator of Portuguese enterprise, had taken Ceuta, the southern gate of the Straits of Gibraltar: and the instructions which the government gave to the commanders who led the way to India were 'to begin with preaching, and if that failed to proceed to the sharp determination of the sword[1].' But there was more of the trader in the Portuguese than in the Spanish character. They showed their commercial instincts by the odious eagerness with which they followed up the slave trade: more negroes were imported into Brazil than into the Spanish possessions on the mainland of America, and the Portuguese province of Angola was developed with a view to supplying slaves to the New World.

CHAPTER VI.

Their merits as colonisers.

In the eyes of the Spaniards, trade consisted in importing so much gold and silver from America into Spain; but the Portuguese successfully monopolised the general traffic of the East, the pepper of Malabar, the spices and timber of the East Indian islands, the silks of China, and the precious stones of India and Ceylon. Being traders, they did not attempt to do so much as the Spaniards in so short a space of time: they were content for the most part to plant stations on the coast without extending their dominion far inland; they emigrated in large numbers, and colonised the outskirts of the East to a greater extent than the European nations which came in after them.

11. Their rise and decline, however, like those of the Spanish power, were very rapid. During the first part of the sixteenth century they made their empire, during the latter part they were already entering on the downward path. Like the Spaniards, they rose on the tide of chivalry, religious fanaticism and adventurous search for riches; and, like the

Their defects.

[1] These were the instructions given to Cabral on his voyage to India in 1500. The words are quoted from Birdwood, 'Report on the India Office Records:' they are given in more detail in the note to p. 184 of 'The Three Voyages of Vasco da Gama,' Hakluyt series.

CHAPTER VI.

Spaniards, they treated the natives with cruelty, and carried into their dependencies political, religious, and commercial oppression.

Goa was the centre of government in the East, it was also the headquarters of the Church and Inquisition. Its splendour and prosperity in the sixteenth century, like that of some of the Brazilian towns at a later period, bore full witness to the capabilities of the Portuguese race. But the despotism of which it was the seat was unscrupulous and corrupt to the last degree, and contained in itself the seeds of inevitable decay.

The monopoly of trade in the Portuguese as in the Spanish Empire was reserved to the Crown, and no chartered companies helped to build up the dominion and to extend the trade of Portugal in the East. At a later date, however, in 1649, and on the other side of the world, a Portuguese Brazil Company was formed under pressure of war with the Dutch[1], and its formation contributed in no small degree to bring that war to a successful issue. While later still, in the middle of the eighteenth century, exclusive privileges of trading with the Brazilian provinces of Maranham and Pernambuco were granted to private companies by the Portuguese minister Pombal.

Special causes of their decline.

12. Among the special causes of the decline of the Portuguese may be noted the fact, that in 1580 the mother country lost her liberty and became a dependency of the Spanish crown—a blow which was fatal to public spirit among her officers abroad, and exposed her possessions to the hostilities of the Dutch[2].

The small size and small population of Portugal must also be borne in mind. Patriotism, which is nowhere so strong as in a small community, does much to encourage

---

[1] See what has been said in previous chapters, and see Watson, 'History of Spanish and Portuguese South America,' vol. ii. chaps. iv. and xv.

[2] See Seeley, 'Expansion of England,' Lecture V.

schemes of enterprise and conquest; but, when a little state has won an Empire, it must either in some sort grow into and become amalgamated with it, or sooner or later be hopelessly overweighted by the size of its dependencies. It was this second evil alternative which befell the Portuguese.

Nor was the policy of the home government in the administration of their dependencies such as to hold together and consolidate an empire. The Viceroys were changed at intervals of three years, changes which were accompanied by corresponding mutations in the subordinate offices[1]; their power was restricted by making them dependent on Councils of advice and control; and the single viceroyalty of the East Indies was broken up into independent governments in opposition to the lines of policy laid down by Albuquerque. In short, the king and his Ministers regarded the officers whom they sent out with jealousy and suspicion; and were served in turn by a set of men who kept the home authorities in the dark as to the true condition of their dependencies; who did not administer justice to the people, but 'only enquired what profit their predecessors derived from their administration that they might obtain more[2];' who made money by trading on their own account, and who were generally speaking worthless and corrupt.

Lastly, in addition to the mistake which the Portuguese, in common with all other European nations, made of crippling their trade by a system of close monopolies, they further erred in not laying themselves out directly to supply the markets of Europe. They brought back the riches of the East to Lisbon only, and left it to the Dutch to distribute them through other European ports. The Dutch thus acquired a large carrying business, which the Portuguese might well have kept in their own hands.

---

[1] See Heeren, 'Political System of Europe and the Colonies;' and Lewis, 'Government of Dependencies,' Note O in Appendix.
[2] Ribeiro, 'History of Ceylon,' translated by Lee, book iii.

74 GEOGRAPHY OF THE COLONIES.

CHAPTER VI.

General results.

13. The Portuguese race, like the kindred Spanish race, was wanting in capacity for progress; and while superior to the Spaniards in some points, they were not their equals in administration; they lost the bulk of their Eastern possessions long before Spain lost her American Empire; and they left on record no evidence of a definite system, which, however faulty, might have acted as a bond to hold together their dependencies.

Dutch colonisation. Dutch contrasted with Spaniards and Portuguese.

14. When we turn from the Portuguese to the Dutch, we come to a new phase of colonisation. The work is now taken up by one of the northern nations of Europe, and by a people of the Teuton breed, embodying the spirit of opposition to political and religious despotism, a trading and seafaring race. The struggle between Spain and Holland was a struggle between Latin and Teuton, between absolutism and democracy, between Roman Catholic and Protestant, between continental Imperialism and a people who sought for trade not for empire, who looked to the sea not to the land, and who represented the rise of the middle class in the modern social system, as opposed to the old monarchy, church, and aristocracy.

As the Spaniards and Portuguese were trained to conquer and colonise by their wars with the Moors, so the prelude to the great part, which the Dutch played in the colonisation of the world, was their long and eventually successful struggle against Philip of Spain for the political and religious independence of their country, a fight in which, to a degree unique in history, they owed their safety to the sea.

Extent and nature of the Dutch colonial empire.

15. It has been seen that Spain and Portugal divided the world between them, and any intrusion of the Spaniards into the East or of the Portuguese into the West was more or less accidental. But the nations which came after had not an open field; they could not confine themselves to one quarter of the globe and remain there unmolested; wherever they went they were regarded as interlopers, and so Dutch, French, and

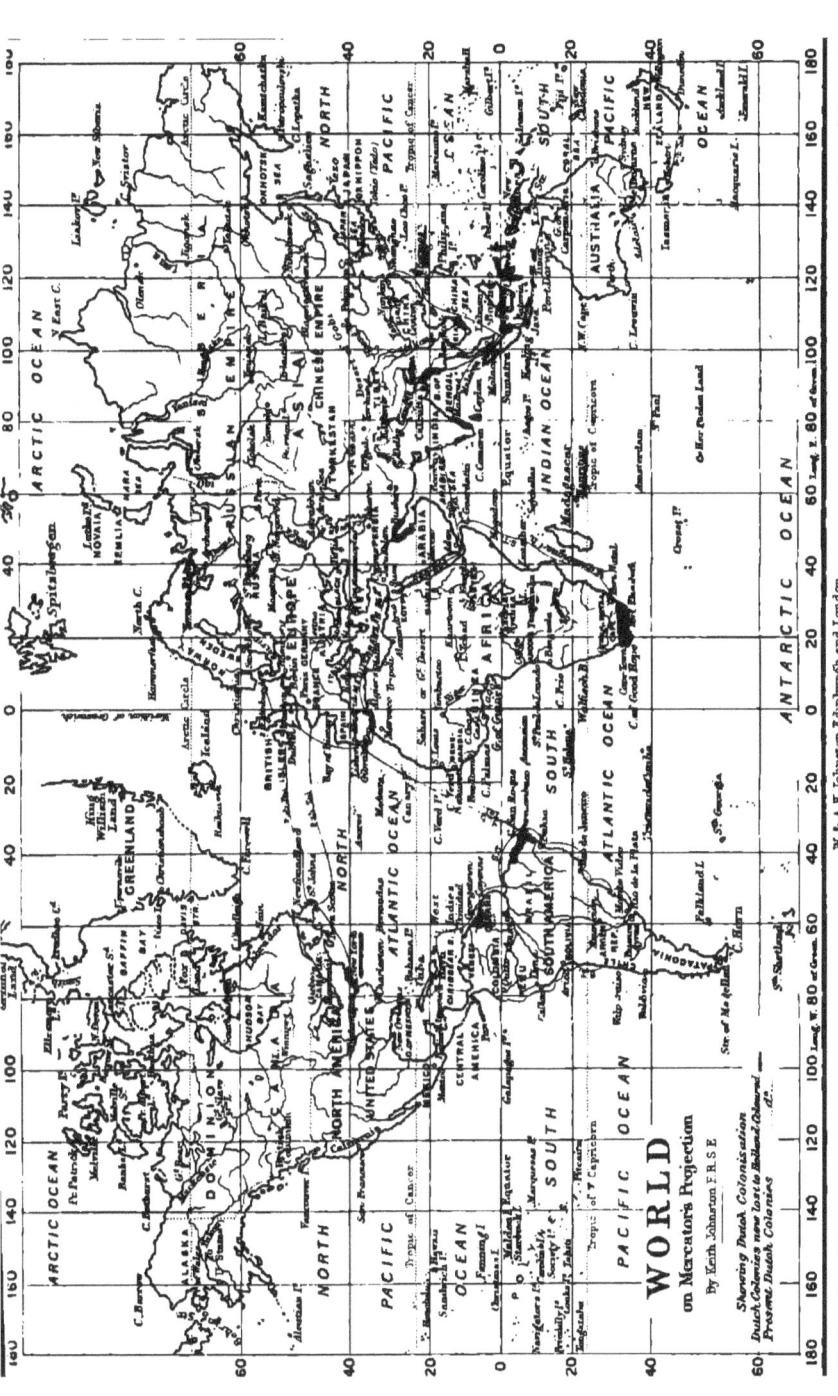

English alike fought, conquered, and colonised both in East and West. The Dutch however followed mainly in the steps of the Portuguese; their successes were more brilliant in the East than in the West; and, unlike the Portuguese, they retained a more permanent hold on Asia than on America. Their rise, as a colonising nation, dates from the beginning of the seventeenth century; their great East India Company being incorporated in 1602. The eighty years from 1661 to 1741 are given as the period of their greatest fortune and power in the East[1]. By 1661 they had practically driven their Portuguese rivals out of the Indian seas. They had taken Mauritius and St. Helena; had planted a colony at the Cape; and had established factories on the shores of the Persian Gulf, in the Persian capital of Ispahan, along the Malabar and Coromandel coasts of India, in Bengal, in Burmah and Cochin China. They had expelled the Portuguese from Ceylon, Malacca, and Formosa, and killed their trade with China and Japan. They had become all-powerful in the East Indian Islands, the possession of which with their rich trade was the earliest, as it was always the main, object of all Dutch efforts; and, as far back as 1619, they had founded in Java the great city of Batavia, the capital of Netherlands India[2]. They had explored too, while they traded and conquered, and made known to the world, Australia, Tasmania, and New Zealand[3].

CHAPTER VI.

The East.

Such was their work in the East. Meanwhile Hudson, who had been sent out by the Dutch East India Company

The West.

---

[1] See Birdwood, 'Report on the India Office Records,' p. 72.
[2] See 'Voyage of Linschoten to East Indies,' published by the Hakluyt Society. In this book, which was issued in 1595-6, he advised his countrymen to go to Java, because they would there not come into collision with the Portuguese.
[3] See what is said in the next chapter; and see Birdwood's account of the first discoverers of Australia in his 'Report on the India Office Records.' He says the 'first practical discovery' of Australia was made by the Dutch, p. 73.

CHAPTER VI. to carry on the vain search for a north-west passage to India, in 1609 sailed up the American river which still bears his name. In 1621 the Dutch West India Company was incorporated, with exclusive rights to trade and colonise in America and on the West Coast of Africa: and in 1622, within three years from the founding of Batavia, the settlement of New Amsterdam was planted, where the city of New York now stands. The English element in America however proved too strong for the Dutch, and in 1674, the province of New Netherlands, as it was then called, was finally transferred to England and became the state of New York. The main object of the Dutch West India Company however was not to colonise North America, but to invade Brazil. The first Dutch fleet sailed for Brazil at the end of 1623, and for some thirty years the north-east coast of the country, including the province of Pernambuco, was in Dutch hands. The Brazilians however gave the invaders no rest, but fought them steadily year after year, until in 1654 they finally drove them out of their territory. It was during this period of war in Brazil, that the Dutch acquired a footing on the West Coast of Africa, taking from Portugal her fort of Elmina; and secured the West Indian Islands, which they still hold, the largest, Curacao, having been a Spanish colony. Their possessions in Guiana, of which they still retain Surinam, date from the year 1666.

The Portuguese were not, as the Spaniards were, the natural foes of the Dutch: indeed Portugal and Holland had several points of similarity to each other, in the smallness of the home territory, and in the trading and seafaring instincts of the people: but it was nevertheless the Portuguese, rather than the Spaniards, whom the Dutch supplanted in foreign parts. This result was due partly to the Portuguese empire becoming subject to the Spanish government; partly to the nature of the Portuguese dependencies, which were more attractive to a people seeking for footholds for trade than the great continental dependencies of Spain; and partly to the rivalry, which would naturally spring up between two sets of traders, and which was repeated between the Dutch and English.

16. The keynote of Dutch colonisation was trade. The commercial character of the Netherlanders was shown in the fact, that they were the chief carriers of Europe before they took to colonising: indeed their attacks on the Portuguese possessions orginated in their being threatened with the loss of the carrying trade though the annexation of Portugal by Spain. Their dealings too with the peoples of the East were the dealings of merchants, not of warriors or conquerors: they did not lord it among them in the fashion of the Portuguese [1], but put up with every form of insult and outrage from the native kings so long as their trade was not interfered with: they guided their policy for good and ill by the interest of their commercial monopoly: and, while staunch supporters of the reformed religion, subordinated religion itself to trade [2]. 'Churches were built in Ceylon because the extension of the Protestant faith was likely to counteract the influence of the Portuguese Roman Catholics, and the spread of Christianity to discourage the Moors and Mohammedan traders:' and in North America, while England in her patents made the conversion of the natives a prominent purpose, the Dutch were chiefly intent on promoting trade [3].'

Trading instincts of the Dutch.

The monopolies of the Latin peoples were, as we have seen, almost entirely crown monopolies: the Dutch, on the other hand, committed their trade wholly to chartered companies. In the dealings of these companies commercial exclusiveness

Dutch East India Company.

---

[1] See Emerson Tennent, 'Ceylon,' Part 6, chap. ii.
[2] Ibid.
[3] See Bancroft, 'History of America,' chap. xv. In the sketch of Formosa, referred to above, it is shown that the Dutch government discouraged the conversion of the natives in that island in order to conciliate the Japanese with whom they were trading.

was carried to the last extreme: the trade of the Spice Islands especially was most jealously and unscrupulously protected from foreign interference, as shown by the massacre of English traders at Amboyna in 1622; and most carefully and minutely regulated. The system was at once ungenerous, oppressive, and unsound, but it had the merit, which Motley points out[1], of concentrating 'the private strength and wealth of the mercantile community'—a species of concentration which was necessary while Holland was fighting her way up among nations, and which, as has been noted, Portugal subsequently adopted against her in Brazil with much success.

The Dutch East India Company might not have been so successful or retained its success so long, but that it was so steadily and strongly backed by the government: it practically represented the state in its dealings with the East, and the policy of the government towards it was consistent and unvarying. In this respect the Dutch Company has been contrasted with the French East India Companies, which were victimised by the constant interference of different kings and ministers with ever-changing views[2]; and also with the English East India Company, which received but a half-hearted and lukewarm support from the English government. But enterprising as the Dutch were, they remained little more than traders from first to last. We have seen that they never emigrated in great numbers; their possession of Ceylon for instance has been described[3] as 'a military tenure not a civil colonisation in the ordinary sense of the term,' and they left no such permanent mark upon the island as the Portuguese, whose influence there may be traced at the present day to a far greater extent in religion, breed, and nomenclature. The two parts of the world where they did not merely trade,

---

[1] 'History of United Netherlands,' chap. xl.
[2] See 'Essay on East India Trade, and comparison of Dutch, French, and English East India Companies,' dated 1770.
[3] In Tennent's 'Ceylon,' Part 6, chap. ii.

but also settled and colonised, viz. the Cape and North America, passed into English hands, and even at the Cape a considerable proportion of the settlers were not Dutch but Huguenot refugees[1]. Nor were they a governing race in the true sense; they governed almost solely with a view to making a direct profit for the mother country, and the Dutch East India Islands are still simply tributary dependencies from which Holland derives so much annual revenue. Yet, merchants as they were, they showed some signs of being qualified to rule. They left behind them a legacy of Dutch law, as in Ceylon, the Cape, and Guiana; and their curiously restricted and non-progressive administration of the East Indian Islands has, on the assumption of the absolute superiority of the European race and the absolute inferiority of the native, resulted in a great degree of prosperity.

17. Among the causes of the success of Dutch colonisation in past time, writers have noticed their strict attention to business, involving dogged maintenance of their commercial monopolies; the rigid supervision kept over their subordinate officers; and the combination in the case of the latter of regular payment and systematic promotion with absolute prohibition of private trading[2]. In these respects they stand out in contrast to the Portuguese: they were more honest and more systematic in their dealings; at the same time they treated the natives with greater humanity. Apart too from the respective characters of the two peoples, the Dutch gained by coming after the Portuguese, just as the English gained by coming after the Dutch: the natives, who hated all foreign interference, naturally hated most their masters for the time being; so the new comers were welcomed as in some sort deliverers and friends. Further, the Dutch were

Causes of Dutch successes.

---
[1] See however Theal, 'Chronicles of Cape Commanders' (chap. xiv), where it is stated, that at the Cape 'at no time did the French exceed in number one sixth of the colonists or one eighth of the whole European population, the company's servants included.'
[2] See Heeren, 'Political System of Europe and the Colonies.'

CHAPTER VI.

well aware of the danger of undue extension of empire, and were carried beyond the limits of their power as a trading nation by force of circumstances, not by their own inclinations. Their likeness to the Carthaginians of old in partiality for island settlements has already been noticed[1], and the Netherlands Indies at the present day are a collection of island dependencies.

Causes of their decline.

18. Their decline was natural. Many causes have been assigned for it, constant little wars with the natives, English competition, decay of the energy which had formed and sustained their great trading companies—decay which was evidenced in the constant change of governors and in the corruption of too poorly paid subordinate officials[2]. But the simple account of their decline is, that their commercial system was unprogressive and unsound, and that they themselves, instead of growing out of the merchant stage, fell back more and more into the position of mere traders.

The political history of the Netherlands too had much to do with the decline of the Dutch power abroad. Holland was a confederation of states, united for purposes of defence against a common foe and to prosecute a foreign trade, which, as the Dutch merchants saw, could only be carried on successfully by combination. To maintain an empire a stronger central government was needed than the United Provinces possessed; and when the defect was partially remedied by making the Stadholdership hereditary in the House of Orange, the good effects of the change were neutralised by the country becoming involved in the political complications of Europe.

General results.

19. Holland was carried by the tide of history and by the strong character of her inhabitants to a place far beyond

---

[1] See chap. v.
[2] See Emerson Tennent, 'Ceylon,' and Lord Valentia's 'Travels, 1802-1806,' to which Tennent refers. In chap. vi. the latter points out the faults of the Dutch administration in Ceylon.

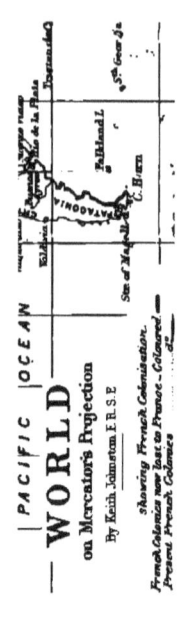

that to which it would at first sight seem nature had assigned her, and she could only retain that place by growing out of herself[1], by broadening the basis of her pyramid, and merging the home country in a Netherlands empire. Like Portugal she failed to do so: she remained throughout her history simply the landlord of a large and profitable estate in foreign parts. But her failure, such as it was, was really the outcome of the deliberate policy of the Dutch government and the Dutch nation. No people ever had so definite an aim in foreign and colonial policy as the Dutch, and none ever realised their aim more completely. From the first their one object was to secure the trade of the Spice Islands. They tried to avoid collision with other powers[2], they did not want to conquer, they did not want to acquire territory, they wanted only to trade. And when in 1824, after the Napoleonic wars, Holland, having become a political cypher in Europe, and having lost Ceylon and the Cape, gained by treaty with England recognition of her possessions in the East Indian archipelago, the object with which she became a colonial power was finally attained.

The Netherlands Indies at the present day, including Java, part of Sumatra, the Moluccas, Celebes, districts in Borneo and New Guinea, and various other smaller islands, form a splendid and prosperous colonial inheritance; and, when compared with the miserable remnants of the Portuguese empire in the East, are conclusive evidence of the superiority in history of Jacob to Esau, of the sober-minded, somewhat mean, Dutch traders to their more showy and chivalrous predecessors of the Latin race.

20. France, like Spain and unlike Portugal and Holland, has filled the place in history of a great continental power, and her career in the field of colonisation has been that

French colonisation. French compared with Spaniards and Dutch.

---

[1] See Seeley, 'Expansion of England,' Lecture V.
[2] See the note on Linschoten given above.

CHAPTER VI.

of a nation seeking for empire, rather than of a commercial people bent on quietly planting settlements and by slow degrees extending its trade.

Dutch history embodies the rise of the middle classes: but when we pass to France, we seem, in coming back to a Latin or mixed Latin race, to turn again in some measure to the despotism which formed the groundwork of the Spanish system. French despotism, however, was of a more modern type than Spanish. The Bourbon kings and their ministers, Sully, Richelieu, Mazarin, Colbert, who held absolute sway in France during the seventeenth and eighteenth centuries, when she was competing for the headship among conquering and colonising nations, were little leavened by the half-savage crusading spirit of the Middle Ages. Their system was a system of modern diplomacy, modern warfare, and modern imperialism, more human than that which it superseded, but almost if not quite as unscrupulous.

Rivalry between France and England.

As France in some sort took the place of Spain, so England gradually took the place of Holland; and the later history of colonisation is the history of the rivalry between these two Western powers.

Extent and nature of French colonial empire.

21. The French owned no colonial possessions before the seventeenth century, although Cartier entered the Gulf of St. Lawrence as early as 1534, and although two unsuccessful Huguenot settlements were planted in Brazil and Florida in 1558 and 1562 respectively [1].

1604 was the date of the founding of Port Royal or Annapolis in Nova Scotia, and in 1608 Champlain founded Quebec. French colonists settled in the West Indian islands of Guadaloupe and Martinique in 1635. About the same date settlements were attempted at Cayenne in Guiana and on the Senegal river in North Western Africa.

In the East, French colonisation or rather French interference was later than in the West, although a French East

[1] See Doyle, 'English in America,' vol. i. chap. v.

India Company was formed as early as 1604. The first CHAPTER VI.
possession actually secured by France in the eastern seas
was the island of Bourbon, now known as Réunion, which
was formally annexed in 1649; but attempts[1] had some
years before been made to form a French settlement in
Madagascar, which island it was hoped might prove a second
Java, and for which the French have ever since shown
a great hankering.

The first French settlement in India was a trading agency
at Surat, established in 1668; and the first place in the great
peninsula which was ceded to France was Pondicherry,
occupied in 1674. By this time Colbert's able commercial
and colonial policy had begun to bear fruit, and the French
power was gradually built up alike in Asia and America, to
be broken a century later after hard fighting by Clive and
Wolfe.

22. The most noticeable point in the foreign and colonial *The French government and the French nation.*
history of the French is that they have constantly been on the
point of carrying all before them, and yet, on each occasion,
have broken down just at the last from what at first sight
appear to be almost accidental causes. Under Louis XIV,
and under the great Napoleon, they were all but masters of
Europe. In the eighteenth century they nearly held America,
and nearly conquered India. They were perpetually served by
great statesmen and soldiers at home and abroad, but the
fruits of the greatness and foresight were as perpetually lost.

The successive failures of the French are attributed by
historians to the bad policy and mismanagement of their
rulers: and though every nation must be held responsible for
the kind of government which it produces or to which it
submits, yet it is true that the history of France beyond that
of any other country can be read aright only by constantly
distinguishing between the people and the government.

---

[1] The first attempt was apparently made in 1642 or perhaps in 1635.
See Raynal, bk. iv.

23. The French, it has been seen, have in many respects always been eminently suited for colonising. They have never been found wanting, in enterprise, in fighting qualities, or power of adapting themselves to new peoples and new countries. Their history, in the East and West alike, proves that they reached a point far beyond that of merely intermarrying with Indians, and falling in with native ways and savage modes of life. Their leaders showed a definite policy in dealing with the native races, they treated them with humanity and consideration, they organised them and gave them cohesion, they formed alliances and counter-alliances, and carried the spirit of European politics into Asia and America. Such were the dealings of Dupleix in India, of Champlain at one time and Montcalm at another in Canada. To quote Mr. Parkman's words in his comparison of the English and French in America [1]:—'The scheme of English colonisation made no account of the Indian tribes; in the scheme of French colonisation they were all in all.'

In other respects too the French people gave evidence of being successful colonisers. Their first connexion with the New World was that of traders pure and simple. Breton and Norman sailors [2] were among the earliest visitors to the North American coasts, and the merchant seamen of St. Malo took the lead in *bona fide* commerce between Europe and the New World. They went out not to conquer or to look for gold, but to follow up the fisheries of Newfoundland and the fur trade of Canada. Starting with commercial objects, they steadily settled in Canada; they made no showy and rapid conquest, but quietly worked to make America French. They took their way up the St. Lawrence and down the Ohio, to join the settlement, which in 1684 La Salle placed at the mouth of the Mississippi.

[1] In the 'Pioneers of France in the New World.'
[2] See Doyle, 'English in America,' vol. i. chap. v. In 1527 twelve French ships were found together at the Newfoundland fisheries.

And, when finally conquered, they left the present province of Quebec to be to all times evidence of solid French colonisation.

The first French colonies, again, in the West Indian Islands were not formed or even countenanced by the government, though subsequently bought up by Colbert. They were purely the result of individual enterprise, of the efforts of adventurers and buccaneers, who played for their own hand, attacked the monopoly of the Spanish main, and succeeded to such an extent that St. Domingo, one of the points at which they established themselves, was, prior to the French Revolution, the most thriving of all the islands.

24. What, then, were the failings of the government which in the end more than counterbalanced the aptitude of the people for colonisation? The commercial regulations were not at fault, for though, like other governments, the French under Colbert's guidance sanctioned a regular system of colonial monopolies, entrusting the trade of the colonies to chartered companies, in other respects, as far as commerce was concerned [1], they were more enlightened and liberal in their colonial policy than their neighbours. There was no jealous exclusion of foreigners from French possessions: colonial matters were supervised by a council of commerce, in which the chief manufacturing towns of France were represented: and the mother country was taxed for the benefit of her dependencies to a greater extent than was the case in the systems of other nations. The errors of the government, which proved so fatal to the empire, were not commercial, but partly political and partly religious. Politically they made two mistakes: in the first place they tried to do too much; in the second place they wanted a settled, a continuous, and a reliable policy. As regards the first point, Professor Seeley[2] points out that France had too many irons in the fire, that

Chapter VI.

Causes which led to failure of French colonisation.

Faults of the government.

Want of definite policy.

---

[1] See Burke, 'European Settlements in America.'
[2] 'Expansion of England,' Lecture V.

her European policy was fatal to her colonial empire, and that 'she lost the New World because she was always divided between a policy of colonial extension and a policy of European conquest.' Similarly Professor Freeman[1] shows that 'the time of the greatest power of France in Europe' (the end of the last and the beginning of the present century) 'was by no means equally favourable to her advance in other parts of the world;' and that while she conquered her neighbours on the Continent, she lost her dependencies abroad. It need hardly be added that the same fault of taking up too much at once has been conspicuous in French foreign policy in late years.

To take illustrations of the second point, we have seen that, as compared with the Dutch, the French government perpetually interfered with their chartered companies, instead of giving them a steady consistent support. The absence of a continuous policy is shown by the fact that there were no fewer than six distinct French East India Companies, the first incorporated in 1604, the sixth in 1719. At times the government proved directly faithless to the nation, as in 1565, when it paid no heed to and probably actually connived at the savage massacre by the Spaniards of Ribault's colony in Florida, leaving the honour of France to be avenged by the arms of a private adventurer, Dominic de Gourges. The efforts of a farsighted if sometimes mistaken minister like Colbert, who devoted his energies to strengthening the commerce and the colonies of his country, were rendered fruitless by the caprices and extravagances of Louis XIV and his court: and, in the reign of his worthless successor, intrigues at home resulted in the absence of a strong and honest policy abroad. Court favourites were appointed to high commands, corruption and peculation were rife among the subordinate officers, and even where there were capable men at the head of affairs, ruinous dissensions and jealousies

---

[1] 'Historical Geography of Europe,' chap. ix.

sprang up and were fostered between them, as between Dupleix and Labourdonnais in the East, and between Montcalm and Vandreuil in Canada[1].

CHAPTER VI.

26. But if the political mistakes of the French government were great, its attitude in the matter of religion was even more fatal to the strength and permanence of the French colonial empire. French colonisation was in its origin in great measure the work of the Huguenots, who formed no small portion of the industrial classes of France, and who numbered in their ranks the sailors and merchants of the west coast. Yet, as we have seen, when the Huguenots in the sixteenth century settled in Brazil and Florida, they were neglected or betrayed by the French government. In 1685 they were driven out of France by the revocation of the Edict of Nantes; and they were deliberately excluded from Canada, the one part of the world which, greatly through their instrumentality, bade fair to become in fact as in name New France.

Religious exclusiveness.

When in 1627 Richelieu incorporated the company of the 100 associates to carry on the colonisation of Canada, one of the terms of the charter of incorporation was, that no Huguenot should be allowed to settle there; and, through the influence of the Jesuits, this suicidal policy was steadily maintained as long as Canada remained a French possession.

Persecuted creeds were sure to find a refuge in one or other of the English colonies; but the religious control of the Canadians was placed absolutely in the hands of Jesuit missionaries or of French priests[2], whose bigotry, in Acadia at least, was by the testimony of their own countrymen the main cause of the sufferings and misery of the settlers during the struggle between England and France. The judgment of history is that France lost Canada through the policy of

[1] See Parkman, 'Montcalm and Wolfe.'
[2] Ibid. chaps. i. and viii.

88 GEOGRAPHY OF THE COLONIES.

CHAPTER VI.

religious exclusiveness which her rulers pursued. Nor can it be supposed that the effects of this policy ended here. Though the large majority of Frenchmen professed the Roman Catholic faith, measures of intolerance which drove from France her most industrious citizens, and which blighted the progress and caused the loss of her most promising colony, must necessarily have widened the gulf between the French government and the French people, and made it clear, if evidence were wanted, that the policy of the court was opposed to the interests of the nation.

Want of harmony between the government and the nation.

27. The evils of a despotic government may be to some extent discounted, if it reduces all classes of its subjects to the same political and social level; but this redeeming feature was wanting under the despotism of the Bourbons. The laws, the administration, and the social system of France during their reigns were such as to favour the aristocratic classes at the expense of the general community; and the inequalities which pressed so hardly upon the lower orders, and which finally gave birth to the French revolution, were not confined to the mother country, but were perpetuated in the colonies. The result was seen in Canada. Once conquered by the English, the Canadian people tasted greater liberty and felt the benefit of more democratic institutions[1]. They were given a just criminal law, and were allowed to retain their old civil rights and customs and their old religion. Though but sixteen years after the conquest of Canada the revolt of the United States gave them a most favourable opportunity for rising against their English masters, they showed no disposition to upset the new order of things: they rested contented with an alien rule, and practically gave out to the world that their own French government—selfish, corrupt, and out of sympathy with national growth and progress—had shown itself unfitted to maintain and develop a great colonial system.

[1] See Raynal, 'East and West Indies,' bks. xvi. and xvii.

28. In spite, however, of the loss of their dependencies in the last century, the French at the present day fill a very different position among colonising nations from that of the Spaniards or Portuguese. France is still a power and a forward power in all parts of the globe, conquering rather than settling, and still as of old interfering in too many places at once. She yet holds Pondicherry and some other small stations in India: she yet keeps Réunion by the side of Mauritius, which England has taken from her; Guadaloupe, Martinique and Cayenne in the West Indies, the islets of St. Pierre and Miquelon off the coast of Newfoundland, Senegal on the West Coast of Africa, are remains of her former colonial possessions; while in Algeria and Tunis on the Northern Coast of Africa, at the Gaboon river in Equatorial Africa, in Cochin China, in Madagascar, in New Caledonia, Tahiti, and other islands in the Pacific, she has been and still is using every effort to build up a new colonial empire.

CHAPTER VI.

French colonies at the present day.

CHAPTER VII.

ENGLISH COLONISATION.

Chapter VII.

English colonisation.

1. ENGLAND closes the list of great colonising nations, for the Danes and Swedes hardly stand in the first rank as colonisers: the Germans have sent out their emigrants to be the subjects of foreign governments, and have as yet formed but few and unimportant colonial dependencies of their own: and the expansion of the Russian power, though parallel to that of the Roman, is not as a rule regarded in the light of colonisation.

Its success due to the country and the race.

The great success of the English, at once in planting colonies and in retaining them when planted, must be mainly attributed to the character of the country and the race.

Main features of Great Britain and its inhabitants.

2. Great Britain stands alone in Europe in being an island power. For over[1] two hundred years she has had no part or lot in the continent of Europe; and the one geographical fact of being bounded on all sides by the sea accounts, as writers have times without number pointed out, for the special course taken by English history.

The insular position of England has made the English a race of sailors. It has given the country a temperate climate, far more favourable to systematic effort than the more intense heat and cold of inland countries in the same latitude. Most of all, it has kept the people from being

---

[1] Practically since the loss of Calais in 1558. Dunkirk, however, was held from 1658-1663.

perpetually entangled, like their French neighbours, in foreign troubles, leaving them free to develop and extend their commerce and empire in Europe and the East.

The British Isles stand out, as the westernmost, spur of Europe, on the way to the New World. Their position at first sight is not equally favourable to commerce with the East; but it must be borne in mind that throughout modern history the trade and colonisation of the far East and far West have been closely bound up together. The one object of early enterprise towards America was to discover a route to the Indies. Dutch and English sailors tried again and again to find a short cut to the Indian seas by north-east and north-west passages; and, from the beginning of the sixteenth century to the opening of the Suez Canal, the main road, by which the commerce of Europe and Asia was interchanged, was the ocean road round the Cape of Good Hope, open only to the fleets of those countries which looked out upon the Atlantic.

Inferior in area to France or Spain, the British Isles are nearly ten times the size of Holland and between three and four times that of Portugal; they are therefore proportionately better able than the two last-named countries to stand the strain of imperial extension. Small as these islands are compared with other lands, a study of the map shows at once that their geography is far from being uniform, and that within a limited space are to be found striking varieties of physical feature, climate and productions. The mountains of the north and west contrast with the low-lying eastern counties and with the open southern downs: the climate of the Scotch Highlands is far removed from that of the Isle of Wight or South Devon: and the manufacturing and mineral districts of Lancashire and Yorkshire are a different world from the Weald of Kent.

Again, though surrounded by the sea, Great Britain is the most accessible of islands. The coasts are indented with

CHAPTER VII.

broad estuaries running far inland, which invite visitors and commerce from all quarters. Hence in the early days of restless migration England was not left to herself, and many streams from many lands have combined to give her a mixed population. The English-speaking breed is one composed of various elements, English, Saxons, Jutes, Danes, Northmen, Flemings; while the Welsh, the Irish, the Manx, and the Northern Scotch, are offshoots, and distinct offshoots, of the Celtic stock. In short, there is no more sameness in the inhabitants of these islands than there is in the home which they inhabit. Differences of race too have been accompanied by varieties of religion; for the line is sharply drawn between the English Episcopalian, the Scotch Presbyterian, the Welsh Methodist, and the Irish Roman Catholic.

These diversities of geography, of breed, and religious thought, give some clue to the history of the English as a colonising nation. The sea bade them colonise, and as colonisation takes men into various parts of the earth, and places them in ever varying circumstances, it seems to follow that the inhabitants of a country, which is a miniature world in itself, will be more successful colonisers than those whose land and breed and thought are all of one uniform type.

Though the Celts have played no unimportant part in the history of Great Britain, the position which this country has won in the world has been won mainly by and in the name of the English-speaking race.

The prominent physical characteristics of this mixed breed, due in no small degree to the influence of climate, are strength, endurance, and reproductiveness. Their chief mental qualities are independence and self-reliance; a dislike of extremes, whether in the natural or in the political or religious world; a love of law, order, and system; and a capacity for progress, for permanently if slowly widening in ideas. If to any stock more than another has been given the mission to be 'fruitful and multiply, to replenish the earth and subdue it,' history seems to tell that such has been the calling of the children of England. And in an age when the hitherto hidden forces of coal and iron have been called into play, it is not wonderful that the people which found them ready to hand, and earliest learnt to use them, have thereby increased their lead among the nations of the world.

CHAPTER VII.

3. It has been said that the English come last in the list of colonising peoples, and it is true that in founding settlements and in acquiring territory beyond the seas they were at first outstripped by other European nations.

Early English explorers.

At the same time, England was worthily represented in early maritime enterprise. The Venetian Sebastian Cabot set out from Bristol, commissioned by Henry VII, only five years after Columbus started on his first voyage: and the record of the sixteenth century is rich with the names of bold adventurers, who set forth from English ports to search out the dark places of the world.

Among them were de Prado and Hore; the Arctic explorers Willoughby and Chancellor, who sailed in search of a north-east passage to the Indies, and Frobisher and Davis, who went to the north-west; Hawkins, the business-like slave-trader; the daring freebooter Sir Francis Drake, who taught Englishmen to laugh at the power of Spain and the terrors of the Inquisition, and who almost in defiance of his own government led his Devonshire men into every corner of the globe; Cavendish, who repeated Drake's exploit of sailing round the world; the high-souled Humphrey Gilbert, who died as he lived in the fear of God alone; and his brilliant half-brother Sir Walter Raleigh, statesman, courtier, and knight-errant. These and others like them made England a power in the maritime world, and accustomed her sailors to the dangers alike of the frozen seas and of the tropics.

A literature of geographical discovery too sprang up in England, in which Richard Hakluyt's is not the first though it is the greatest name[1]. Early in the century Henry VIII founded three colleges for the encouragement of scientific seamanship. By 1540 the fisheries of Newfoundland[2] had become so important to this country as to be specified in an Act of Parliament. When the seventeenth century opened with the formation of companies to follow up the East Indian trade, the first national East India Company was the English, incorporated on the last day of the year 1600, and senior by two years to the Dutch East India Company, by four years to the French.

Lateness of English colonisation compared with that of other races.

4. But, bold and energetic as were the English voyagers of the sixteenth century, their enterprise produced at the time no tangible result. For a century and more after the first discovery of the New World and the rounding of the Cape of Good Hope, the English people were merely training themselves for the coming time. Spain and Portugal had made their colonial empires, and were beginning to decay, before our fathers had planted a single settlement or won a single colonial dependency. The Dutch secured a foothold in the East and possessed themselves of the rich heritage of the Portuguese, while English trading vessels were still slowly and painfully finding their way into the Indian seas. The French outpaced us in North America. It was only after long years of hard struggle that English colonisation in the West, deriving its strength and solidity from independence of the home government, proved its superiority to the work of rival countries; and English merchants in the East Indies showed that private enterprise is surer if slower in its results than efforts directed by and relying on the state.

5. The sixteenth century then was the time of training, and

---

[1] The dates of the principal voyages are roughly as follows:—Cabot, 1497; de Prado, 1527; Hore, 1536; Willoughby, 1553; Chancellor, 1553-6; Frobisher, 1576-8; Davies, 1585-7; Hawkins, 1562-7; Drake, 1572, 1577, etc.; Cavendish, 1586; Gilbert, 1578-83; Raleigh sent out his first expedition in 1584; Hakluyt was born 1553, died 1616, began to publish 1582.

[2] See Doyle, 'History of the English in America,' vol. i. chap. iv.

PACIFIC OCEAN

WORLD
on Mercator's Projection
By Keith Johnston, F.R.S.E.

English Colonies at the end of the 19th Century

with the seventeenth colonisation began. There have thus been nearly three centuries during which the English have been engaged in colonising, and a study of the manner in which the colonial possessions of Great Britain have been acquired will show that each century of colonisation has had a distinct character of its own. Any such comparison however can be only of the most general kind; for in tracing the origin of the English colonies it is often difficult, and sometimes almost impossible, to decide how much should be attributed to cession or conquest and how much to settlement; and when dependencies are said to have been acquired by settlement, the further difficulty arises of determining at what date the first permanent settlers appeared on the scene.

CHAPTER VII.

Three periods of English colonisation. First period the seventeenth century. Results of that period.

Newfoundland claims to be the earliest English colony. Long the resort of English sailors and fishermen, it was formally annexed to Great Britain by Sir Humphrey Gilbert in 1583; but it was not colonised till the following century, when a Bristol company in 1610, and Lord Baltimore[1] in 1623, attempted to form settlements in the island, though with slight success; and it was not finally assured to the English empire till the peace of Utrecht in 1713.

Newfoundland.

The unsuccessful Scotch colony planted by Sir W. Alexander in the Acadian peninsula in 1621–23, which left behind it nothing but the name of Nova Scotia, gives some colour for the statement, that this territory was acquired by settlement at that time: but it is safer to date the acquisition from the peace of Utrecht, under the provisions of which Nova Scotia and New Brunswick were made over by France to England.

Nova Scotia.

Barbados is English in virtue of settlement, and unlike most of the West Indies has never changed hands: 1605 is given as the date of its acquisition, but the first English colonists appear to have landed in 1625.

West Indies and Bermudas.

The solitary group of the Bermuda Islands in the North

---

[1] Subsequently the first proprietor of Maryland.

CHAPTER VII.

Atlantic Ocean was annexed in 1609 by Sir G. Somers, who was wrecked there on his way to Virginia, and who has left to the islands their second name[1]: an English settlement is said to have been planted in them in 1611.

Soon afterwards the English claims upon the smaller West Indian Islands began. The settlement of St. Kitts dates from 1623, of Nevis from 1628, of the Bahamas and Turks Islands from 1629, of Antigua and Montserrat from 1632, of Anguilla from 1650, and of the Virgin Islands, where Dutch buccaneers were driven out by English adventurers, from 1666: while in 1655 Cromwell's officers made amends for the failure of their attempt on Hispaniola, by taking the fine Spanish dependency of Jamaica.

West coast of Africa.   The date assigned to the first English settlement at the Gambia is 1631, though a company was formed to open up the trade of this great West African river as early as 1618. In 1661 Cape Coast Castle on the Gold Coast was taken from the Dutch: other points on the coast were subsequently secured by the Royal African Company which was formed in 1672: and in 1651 the East India Company, anxious to find a halting-place in the South Atlantic on their road to the East, took possession of the little island of St. Helena, which the Dutch had already occupied but subsequently abandoned.

St. Helena.

These are the dependencies at present under the Colonial Office, the acquisition of which dates from the seventeenth century. In India but little territory was annexed during the period: it was not till 1689 that the thought of sovereignty[2] was

India.

---

[1] The Bermudas are mentioned by Shakespeare in The Tempest, Act I. Scene ii.:—

'Where once
Thou call'dst me up at midnight to fetch dew
From the still-vex'd Bermoothes.'

The Tempest was first produced in 1611.

[2] See Birdwood, 'Report on the India Office Records,' p. 85. He quotes a resolution of the company passed in 1689, recognising the necessity of looking to territorial revenue as well as to trade.

ENGLISH COLONISATION. 97

entertained by the East India Company; and at the end of the century the English possessions in this quarter of the world consisted only of four stations or factories. viz. Madras, which was acquired in 1639, Bombay in 1661, Fort St. David in 1691, and Calcutta in 1696[1]. Of these Bombay was transferred by the Portuguese government to the English crown as part of the dowry of Catherine, the Portuguese princess whom Charles the Second married, and was a few years afterwards (in 1668) handed over to the East India Company; while the other three stations were granted, leased, or sold to the Company by their native owners.

CHAPTER VII.

The chief event of the century however in the field of colonisation was the founding of the United States, the greatest colony, or series of colonies, which has ever been planted by a single people at one period of their history. The first Virginian settlement dates from 1607. On the first day of that year three ships set sail from England, commissioned by a company of London merchants, which had been formed in the previous year. They carried 143 emigrants, among them John Smith, whose name is so prominent in the early history of Virginia. At the end of April they landed in Chesapeake Bay; and, on the 13th of May, they fixed their first settlement at Jamestown, called after the worthless king in whose reign such great things were done.

First colonisation of the United States.

On the 6th of September, 1620, the 'Mayflower,' a small ship of 180 tons, set sail for New England, freighted with 100 Puritan emigrants, who exchanged their place of refuge in the Dutch city of Leyden for a more distant exile: and so steadily was the work of colonisation carried on, that before the close of the century the Atlantic coast of North America, from Maine to South Carolina, was in English hands.

6. These were the results of the first century of English colonisation. At home it was a time of civil war and

Special characteristics of English

[1] See Birdwood, 'Report on the India Office Records,' p. 90.

H

CHAPTER VII.

colonisation in the seventeenth century.

revolution, of political and religious oppression, and of political and religious revolt. The government had too much on its hands during the greater part of the period to busy itself with foreign wars and conquests, while private citizens in all grades of society and of all shades of opinion found, some during one régime, some during another, every inducement to emigrate from a country which was passing through a phase of restlessness and discontent.

Under such conditions as these, colonisation took a special course. The age was one in which the individual did much and the state little. It was an age of settlement not of conquest; and hardly any of the dependencies acquired during these years were taken by the sword. Though New York was conquered from the Dutch, the United States are in the main the result of settlement pure and simple. The small possessions secured in India before 1700 were rather of the nature of trading stations, sold or ceded by the native authorities, than the outcome of a definite policy of war and annexation. And of the colonial dependencies which we still hold, as enumerated above, the only one of importance, which was the direct fruit of a struggle with a foreign power, was Jamaica, taken from Spain at a time when Cromwell had established a strong government at home and a strong policy abroad.

As the home government was unable and unwilling to risk much in foreign interference, private citizens learned to combine among themselves for the protection and further-ance of their foreign and colonial trade. So the century was marked by the formation and the growth of private companies. Various American companies came into existence, the Virginia, the Plymouth, the Massachusetts, and, at a later date, the Hudson Bay Company. The East India Company was born with the century. The Gambia Company, the Royal African Company, and others, sprang up during its course. Thus early English colonisation went hand in

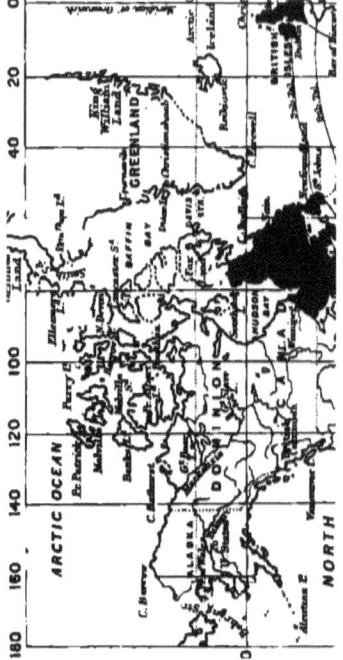

hand with trade rather than with conquest, and was more the result of private venture than of state policy.

The first current of colonisation from Great Britain set mainly towards the West. Although a few English stations were formed in India, it has been seen that no large amount of Indian territory was appropriated during the seventeenth century, and up to its close the colonial dependencies of England were to be found only in North America, in the West Indies, and on the West Coast of Africa.

This Westward tendency was the natural result of the geographical position of the British Isles. But there was a further reason to take English emigrants by preference to the New World. In America there was a temperate climate, ample room for settlers, and comparatively little risk of constant collision with foreign nations: whereas, at all points of the thickly populated East, the merchant and the colonist were brought face to face, in a tropical climate, with native powers far more organised than the unsettled tribes of the Western Continent, and with strong and jealous European nations, which had preceded them in the race for the riches of the Indies.

In short the leading characteristics of English colonial enterprise during the seventeenth century were, that it took the form of settlement rather than of conquest, that it was little interfered with or protected by the state, and that it found its sphere of action chiefly in the West.

7. With the eighteenth century English colonisation entered on a new and widely different phase. This second period, reaching down to 1814, comprises the years during which Great Britain became an Imperial power. It was a time when foreign policy engrossed the attention and the energies of her statesmen: and its record is a record of perpetual warfare with other European nations, especially with France. The dependencies, which England then won, were won chiefly at the point of the sword: and the men, to

Second period of English colonisation, 1700–1814. Its main characteristics. The struggle between France and England.

GEOGRAPHY OF THE COLONIES.

CHAPTER VII.

Loss of United States.

whom they were due, were statesmen and soldiers, not explorers or merchants or pioneers of peaceful settlement. The losses too which the country sustained, no less than its gains, show the special character of the period. The revolt of the United States followed close on the victories of Wolfe in Canada and Clive in India. The time when the greatest of English conquests was won, was the time when the greatest of English settlements was lost; for the spirit of the age, which favoured annexation by the strong arm of the state, ran counter to the feeling of independence, which had inspired the founding, and grown with the greatness, of the North American Colonies.

First half of the period to 1763. Its results.

8. The period can be conveniently divided into two parts. The first closes with the Peace of Paris of 1763. The second with another Peace of Paris in 1814. But the main feature of both epochs was one and the same—the struggle between France and England for the leadership of the world.

Gibraltar.

The first foreign dependency secured by Great Britain during the eighteenth century was Gibraltar, taken from Spain in 1704, the year of the battle of Blenheim. It was the price paid by Spain for her alliance with France in the war of the Spanish succession: and though classed among English colonies, it has been from first to last a mere outpost in a foreign land, a fitting firstfruit of an age, in which it fell to the lot of England to conquer, not to colonise.

West Indies.

Of the West Indian Islands, the peace of 1763 gave to England Dominica in the Leeward group; and St. Vincent, the Grenadines, Grenada, and Tobago, in the Windward; all of which had either actually belonged to France or been claimed by her wholly or in part. The same peace assured the fruits of Wolfe's great victory at Quebec in

Canada.

1759, and transferred the Canadian possessions of France to Great Britain.

Meanwhile, in India as in America, France and England had met each other face to face. But the efforts of Dupleix, Labourdonnais, and Lally, proved eventually as unsuccessful in the East as those of Montcalm in Canada; and the battle of Plassey in 1757, and of Wandewash in 1759, decided, the former that a European race should rule in India, the latter that that race should be the English and not the French. Thus when the climax of the struggle between England and the power of the Bourbon monarchy was reached in 1763, the results of the strife were all in favour of the former. The English were victorious in the East. In the West they held nearly the whole of the North American Continent; and there was little to show, that in twenty years the finest of their American settlements would be lost to them, and that what are now the United States would be permanently severed from the English Crown.

CHAPTER VII.

India.

9. The history of the years from 1763 to 1814 is again roughly a record of war between England and France; the imperialism of the Bourbons being succeeded by that of Napoleon, and the struggle resolving itself more and more into a contest between the first land power and the first sea power of the day. The general result of this second epoch, like that of the first, was to transfer to Great Britain possessions, which either belonged to France, or to powers which had become subordinate to her. Malta was taken from France in 1800. St. Lucia, the last of the Windward group, which, like so many other West Indian Islands, had long been bandied about between the two countries, in 1803. Mauritius, which under the government of Labourdonnais was of great account in the history of the French in the East, in 1810. From Holland England took Ceylon in 1795, the year in which Pichegru reduced the Netherlands to the condition of a French dependency; British Guiana, as it is now called, in 1803; and the Cape, the greatest of Dutch Colonies, in 1806.

Second half of the period, 1763-1814.

Its results.

Malta.

St. Lucia.

Mauritius.

Ceylon.

British Guiana.

The Cape.

CHAPTER VII.

All these dependencies were assured to England by the Peace of Paris in 1814, with the exception of Ceylon, to which the Dutch relinquished their claims under the provisions of the earlier Peace of Amiens in 1802.

Trinidad. The year 1797 saw the surrender of the Spanish island of Trinidad to an English fleet. In 1807 the capture of *Heligoland.* Heligoland from the Danes gave us an outpost in the North sea.

India. Meanwhile in India the English power was rapidly extended at the expense of native rulers and their French allies. The strong policy of Warren Hastings in the earlier years of the period, and of Lord Wellesley in the later, confirmed and broadened the supremacy which had been won by Clive. The Regulation Act of 1772, and Pitt's India Bill of 1784, which established the Board of Control, practically recognised that the time had come for the state to exercise a direct supervision over the great work which was being carried out in the name of a private trading company.

In the Malay Indies the English had from early days competed with the Dutch[1]; but it was only in 1786 that a permanent footing was obtained off the coast of the *Penang.* Malay peninsula. In that year the island of Penang was ceded by the Sultan of Quedah, and formed the nucleus of the still-growing colony of the Straits Settlements.

But though English colonisation in the 18th century was mainly bound up with the foreign complications of the mother country, this account does not hold true of all colonies acquired during these years. For instance, the *British* colony of British Honduras originated in a settlement *Honduras.* which had been formed in that part of Spanish America

---

[1] The massacre of Amboyna in 1623 practically secured to the Dutch the trade of the East Indian archipelago; and in 1684 the English were driven out of Java, but they long retained some positions in the islands, e.g. Bencoolen in Sumatra. See Birdwood as sup.

by private adventurers from Jamaica, who, in spite of Spanish opposition, had carried on for many years a profitable timber trade: and the treaties made with Spain in 1783 and 1786, from which the English claim to this colony dates, were simply a formal recognition of the existing state of things. So also the acquisition of the West African peninsula of Sierra Leone, which in 1787 was ceded to England by its native owners, and shortly afterwards handed over to a company formed for the purpose of suppressing the slave trade, had no connexion with Imperial policy, and was simply an outward and visible sign of the growing antagonism in England to the iniquities of the slave system.

Chapter VII.

Sierra Leone.

Another and more important event in the history of colonisation took place in 1787. Up to the date of the Peace of Paris in 1763, the attention of European nations, when not concentrated on Europe itself, had been directed to the West or the East, to the struggle between France and England in Canada and India. But when the great duel on these two opposite sides of the world had been brought to a temporary close, the restless spirits of the two combatants seemed to look abroad for other fields. Such voyages as those of the Frenchman Bougainville, and the Englishman Cook, both of whom had served in Canada, opened up the Southern ocean; and as soon as England realised that she had finally lost the United States, she forthwith set herself to colonise Australia[1].

First colonisation of Australia.

In the autumn of 1787, the first ship-load of convicts was sent to Australia: they were landed at Botany Bay in the spring of 1788. A detachment was almost immediately sent to Norfolk Island; and in 1803 Tasmania received

[1] Compare the following dates:—Peace of Paris, 1763; Bougainville's voyage round the world, 1766-9; Cook's three voyages, 1769-74; Peace of Versailles, by which England acknowledged the independence of the United States, 1783; First English settlement in Australia, 1788.

CHAPTER VII.

English colonists from the same doubtful source. But though the beginnings of Australian settlement fall within the century of conquest, they must rather be taken as the prelude to the third and last period of English colonisation, dating from the year 1814 to the present day.

Third period of English colonisation, from 1814. Its main characteristics.

10. Since the close of the Napoleonic wars, hardly any acquisition has been made by England, outside the boundaries of India, which can be considered purely in the light of a conquered dependency. The empire has been extended far more by settlement than by conquest: and so far the colonial history of Great Britain in the present century has more in common with the history of the seventeenth century than with that of the intervening age. Yet the difference between the first and third periods is clearly marked. The colonies which date from the seventeenth century are, as has been seen, mainly to be found in the West. In the nineteenth century, on the contrary, though individual emigrants have gone in thousands and tens of thousands to America, yet any actual additions to the Colonial Empire of England have been made rather on the other side of the world.

Again, between 1600 and 1700, the settlements which were formed were due to individual enterprise or the agency of private companies, while in the present age the controlling power of the state has been strongly and directly felt. Though the Australian Colonies are now no state-ridden dependencies, but have developed as vigorous and independent a life as though their earliest founders had been self-exiled Puritans, the fact remains, that the first settlers to Australia were sent out under compulsion by the English Government, seeking for an outlet for the convict population of this country, when no receptacle for criminals could any longer be found in America or the West Indies. While such dependencies as Hong Kong, Fiji, and Cyprus, if not won by the sword, have at least been acquired not through the medium of private adventurers, but by formal cession to the English Crown.

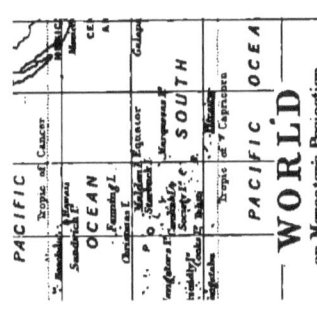

ENGLISH COLONISATION.

Again there is a further contrast to be noticed. In the seventeenth century the world was younger and less explored than in our own time, and the colonies which were then planted were not so much extensions one of another as separate unconnected settlements. During the present century, on the contrary, colonisation has perforce taken more the form of expansion of existing settlements, or of the absorption of conterminous land: an absorption, which in Canada and Australia has been a more or less peaceful process, but which in India and South Africa has been accompanied by constant wars.

CHAPTER VII.

11. Of the smaller dependencies acquired since 1814, the little island of Ascension in the Atlantic to the North of St. Helena was appropriated as a coaling station in 1815. In 1819 the island of Singapore, at the southern end of the Malay peninsula, was secured by treaty with the natives: and, in 1824, the neighbouring Dutch colony of Malacca, which had already in 1795 fallen into English hands, but had been restored to the Netherlands, was finally transferred to England in exchange for Bencoolen, a settlement of the East India Company in the island of Sumatra[1]. In 1833 the southernmost limit of the Empire was reached, possession being taken of the group of the Falkland Islands off the Straits of Magellan, which several powers had in previous years successively occupied and abandoned[2]. In 1838 the rock of Aden, and in 1855 the island of Perim, were added to the list of outposts on the way to India. In 1841 the cession of the then almost uninhabited island of Hong Kong; at the mouth of the Canton river, gave England a footing on the coast of China. In 1846, owing to the efforts of Rajah Brooke, the island of Labuan was taken over from the Sultan of Borneo, though not occupied till two years later. In 1861

Results of the third period.
Ascension.
Singapore.
Malacca.

The Falklands.

Aden and Perim.
Hong Kong.

Labuan.

---

[1] This exchange was the final recognition of English supremacy on the coast of the mainland, and Dutch supremacy in the islands.
[2] The Falkland Islands were first discovered by Davis in 1592.

CHAPTER VII.

Lagos.
Fiji.
Cyprus.

the island of Lagos on the Guinea coast was made over by its native king. In 1874 Fiji became in the same way a British colony. In 1878 Cyprus was occupied under treaty with the Turkish government.

Canadian dominion.

12. To turn to the larger groups of colonies, this century has seen the extension of Canada to the Pacific; and the far-spreading districts, vaguely included in British North America, have been given a substantial existence as provinces of the Canadian Dominion. British Columbia was erected into a Colony in 1858, and in 1871 was incorporated with Canada: Manitoba was constituted a province of the Dominion in 1870: Prince Edward Island, which had been a separate colony since 1770, joined the confederation in 1873: and the North West Territories, which up to the year 1871 had belonged to the Hudson's Bay Company, were given a constitution in 1876. The same process of gradual subdivision and formation of provinces is still being carried out; and, as in the United States, other districts in the North-west are passing through intermediate stages, to be hereafter placed on an equal footing with the older members of the great confederation[1].

Australia.

13. In Australia, the military post stationed by the Governor of Sydney at King George's Sound in 1826, and the Swan River Settlement of 1829, blossomed in due course into the colony of Western Australia. South Australia dates her separate existence as a colony from 1836. Victoria was separated from New South Wales in 1851, and Queensland in 1859. In 1840 the sovereignty of New Zealand was ceded to England by the native chiefs, the cession being followed by an English settlement in 1841.

New Zealand.

South Africa.

14. The colonisation of South Africa has been no easy task, owing to conflicting interests. The work has been

---

[1] In 1882 four provisional districts were cut out of the North-west Territories, viz. Assiniboia, Saskatchewan, Alberta and Athabasca: but they are not at present political units of the Dominion.

ENGLISH COLONISATION. 107

complicated by the presence of Dutch settlers with long established claims, and of a vast native population, not decaying in numbers but holding their own with the white man. Consequently the progress of the English power has here been more faltering than in other parts of the world.

CHAPTER VII.

Natal, the second of the two South African colonies, was settled in 1837 by Dutch emigrants from the Cape: in 1843 it was annexed by the British Government, and, after a period of subordination to the older settlement at the Cape, was in 1856 constituted a separate colony. The territory of Griqualand West, including the diamond fields of Kimberley, came under English rule by right of cession in 1871, and in 1880 was incorporated with the Cape Colony: and the limits of the latter colony have been gradually extended, until on the West Coast they touch the Orange River, and include, besides, the detached port of Walfisch Bay far to the north on the tropic of Capricorn; while on the Eastern side they reach to within almost a hundred miles of the borders of Natal. Outside the boundaries of the two colonies, Basutoland and the southern part of Betshuanaland are now English territory; a vague protectorate is exercised over other outlying districts; and a nominal suzerainty over the South African Republic in the Transvaal.

Natal.

15. The development of the English Empire in India during the century has been almost entirely the outcome of a succession of wars, involving either direct annexation or the indirect subordination of native states under the guise of a protectorate.

India.

The annexation of Scinde in 1 43, and of the Punjaub in 1849, was the result of hard fighting. The possession of the Burmese provinces has been obtained at the cost of three wars, the first taking place in 1824, the second in 1852, and the third in 1885. Oude was annexed by Lord Dalhousie in 1856; and though the annexation was effected by peaceful means, the measure is supposed indirectly to have been one

CHAPTER VII.

of the main causes of the great Indian Mutiny, which followed close upon it[1]. The struggles with the Affghans in 1838–1842 and in 1878–1880, and the other troubled stages in the later history of the English in India, cannot here be traced. It can only be pointed out that, however valuable India may be to Great Britain in point of trade, and whatever advantages the native population may derive from just and systematic rule, yet this great possession has been obtained by force and is held by force, and India has been from first to last purely a conquered dependency. In 1858, after the Mutiny, the policy embodied in Pitt's India Bill was carried out to its conclusion: the Board of Control was superseded by a Secretary of State and Council for India, and all the political rights of the East India Company were transferred to the Crown. Finally the proclamation of the Queen of England as Empress of India—Kaisar-i-Hind—in 1877, may be held to have been an intimation to the world at large, that the suzerainty of the Indian peninsula belongs to England and to England only, and that it has been won and is kept by the force of English arms.

16. It remains to notice the extension of English power, which has lately taken place in the East Indian Archipelago on the border-line between Asia and Australia. English interference in Borneo began with the exploits of Rajah Brooke, who, in 1841, established himself as ruler of the native state of Sarawak with the sanction of the Sultan of the old native kingdom of Brunei. A few years later, he was appointed the first Governor of the little Crown colony of Labuan. Sarawak has, in spite of the wishes of its first ruler,

Sarawak. never been taken over by the English Government, but remains to the present day an independent state, governed by a member of Sir James Brooke's family, and administered by

[1] Owing at least as much to the discontent of the court followers, the aristocracy and the soldiers, who under the native *régime* had battened on the general public, as to the general alarm caused in a very conservative race by a sudden change.

a staff of English officers. Meanwhile the northern peninsula of Borneo had passed into British hands, though not into the keeping of the British Government, having been sold by the Sultan of Brunei to the British North Borneo Company, whose charter of incorporation dates from November 1881.

CHAPTER VII.

British North Borneo.

In New Guinea, under pressure of foreign competition, and in deference to the wishes of the Australians, the home government has interfered more directly than in the case of Borneo: and in 1884 a British protectorate was proclaimed over the south-eastern part of the coast and over the adjacent islands, thereby securing a new field for the future expansion of the Australasian colonies.

New Guinea.

17. Such is a bare chronological outline of the various acquisitions made by Great Britain during her three centuries of colonisation. It remains to describe in a few words the nature of her possessions at the present time in each quarter of the globe.

General results of English colonisation.

In Europe, her foreign dependencies consist of the islands of Heligoland, Malta, Gozo, and Cyprus (which politically, if not geographically, should be included in the European rather than in the Asiatic list), and of the peninsula of Gibraltar.

In Europe.

They must all be classed as military or naval stations. Heligoland is a little stronghold in the Northern Sea, Gibraltar guards the entrance to the Mediterranean, and Malta and Cyprus are further positions on the road to Egypt and the East.

18. In Asia, the area of British rule comprises the peninsula of Aden and the island of Perim; the great peninsula of India, with the Burmese provinces and the outlying island groups of the Andamans, the Nicobars, and the Laccadives; Ceylon, with which the Maldive Islands are nominally connected; the islands of Hong Kong and Labuan; the Straits Settlements, including the two islands of Singapore and Penang, and the territories of Province Wellesley, the Dindings, and Malacca on the main Malay peninsula; and the Keeling Islands, far out

In Asia.

CHAPTER VII.

in the Indian Ocean, now a little dependency of the Straits Settlements. Scattered as these possessions are, they have all a common character. They all consist of peninsulas or islands, for British power and influence in Asia are confined to the outskirts of the continent accessible from the Southern Ocean, and have not penetrated into the great mass of the interior. They are all in or near the tropics. They all must be classed, not as settlements but as dependencies, held either, as India and Ceylon, directly for their own value, or, as the smaller Eastern colonies, partly as military stations, partly as emporia of trade. Aden, for instance, is at once a link in the chain of stations on the way to India and a place of outlet for the Arabian trade. Singapore taps the trade of the Malay peninsula, is a place of junction for Eastern and Australian traffic, and is also an outpost of the empire in the Malay seas. Hong Kong is a half-military, half-commercial station on the borders of the Chinese empire: Labuan a foothold off the coast of Borneo. In these Asiatic dependencies, far more than in any other part of the world, the English have been called to the task of governing native races. To speak of British colonisation in this quarter of the globe is really a misuse of terms: the climate is not for the English breed, and the waste places of the earth are not to be found in the East Indies. The Englishman came to Asia, and has held his ground in Asia, not as a settler, but as a merchant, a conqueror, and a ruler.

In Africa.   19. The British possessions in Africa consist of the Gambia, Sierra Leone, the Gold Coast, Lagos[1], Ascension, and St. Helena; the Cape Colony, with the outlying districts, and Natal; and Mauritius with its dependencies, including the Seychelles Islands, Rodrigues, Diego Garcia, and various other little islands far out in the Indian Ocean.

A reference to the map will show, on the one hand, that in

---

[1] The territory belonging to the Royal Niger Company is also held under a charter from the British Crown.

Africa as in Asia the estate of Great Britain consists almost entirely of islands and peninsulas, and, on the other, that the English have a far greater command of Africa than other European powers; although the French control, or claim to control, a longer extent of coast, and the nominal area of the Portuguese possessions in Africa[1] is much larger than that of the English. The map shows that the dependencies above enumerated form a kind of chain round the continent, which is completed with the help of European and Asiatic stations. Of these latter, Gibraltar gives the key to the entrance to North Africa from the Atlantic; Malta and Cyprus watch from a respectful distance over Egypt and the Suez Canal, which at the present moment are actually in English keeping; while Aden and Perim guard the southern mouth of the Red Sea.

As in Asia the chief English possession is the peninsula of India, so in Africa it is the peninsula of the Cape. But there is this difference between the two; India is and must remain merely a dependency, while the temperate climate of South Africa places the Cape and Natal in the higher category of colonial settlements.

The bulk of the African continent lies within the tropics, and, as might be expected, Europe has invaded Africa chiefly at the northern and southern extremities, which alone are in the temperate zones. To the north the French have been attracted from the opposite coast of the Mediterranean; and here they are trying to build up a colonial empire, though at best it can only be an empire of dependencies, and though for the time being they have lost their hold on Egypt and the Nile.

In the south, England, taking her way over the Atlantic, is the predominant power.

But as the south is more encircled by the sea than the north, the climate is more temperate and better suited to Europeans, or at least to those who hail from the north of

---

[1] See Sir Rawson Rawson's inaugural address to the Statistical Society and his paper on the territorial partition of the coast of Africa in the Magazine of the Royal Geographical Society, November 1884.

Europe, than the climate of the African states which border on the Mediterranean.

In short, while English and French have been rivals in Africa as elsewhere, in Africa as elsewhere the English have secured the better part.

20. In America the British colonies, taken from north to south, are as follows:—Newfoundland, the Canadian Dominion, the Bermudas, the Bahamas, Jamaica and Turks Islands; the Leeward Islands, including Antigua, Montserrat, St. Kitts, Nevis, Anguilla, Dominica, and the Virgin Islands; the Windward Islands, including St. Lucia, St. Vincent, the Grenadines, Grenada, and Tobago; Barbados, Trinidad, British Honduras, British Guiana, and the Falkland Islands.

In America.

As compared with her possessions in Asia, England owns in America a much larger area with an infinitely smaller number of inhabitants. In Asia the heat of the climate is an obstacle to permanent European settlement; in North America settlers have to contend with extreme cold; and a great part of the vast territories of Canada is from this cause uninhabited and uninhabitable. In the East, the English rule an enormous native population; in North America, on the contrary, the native element is insignificant, and the population mainly of European origin: while even in the tropical West Indian Islands, the English breed, favoured by the sea breezes, has taken root and lasted for many generations, forming an exception to the rule that Englishmen cannot make a lasting home in hot climates.

In Asia and Africa, again, English dominion, as has been seen, is confined to the coasts and peninsulas, and has not penetrated far into the continent. It is not so in America. In Canada England holds a distinctly continental empire, which fortunately brings her into contact only with her own children in the United States; while British Honduras and British Guiana are part and parcel of the mainland, and not merely strips of coast or well-defined peninsulas.

ENGLISH COLONISATION.

The English colonies in America are all on the eastern side of the continent, and, except in the Canadian province of British Columbia, they nowhere touch the Pacific coast. The reason of this is not far to seek. Settlements from Europe would in the natural order of things be planted on the side nearest to Europe; and in its geographical formation America looks to the East and turns its back upon the West.

The western coast, from the extreme north to the Straits of Magellan, is lined by the long chain of the Cordilleras and Andes, which shut off the interior from the sea; while on the east are vast plains traversed by great rivers as by high roads, and a coast made accessible by a series of bays and estuaries. Nor can the Pacific shores show any outlying group of islands to match the West Indies, which were placed by nature, and have been used by man, as a convenient starting-point for the colonisation of America.

And, as the English colonies are mainly confined to the eastern side of America, so they are also to be found almost exclusively in the northern half of the continent. In South America the English Empire is represented only by British Guiana at one extremity and the Falkland group at the other.

There is no part of the world, except Australia, which the Anglo-Saxon race has made so completely its own as North America. There is none which it has eschewed so much as South America, partly on account of the heat of the climate, partly because the Latin family had already taken it for its heritage.

21. The Australasian colonies of Great Britain consist of the five divisions of Australia, viz. New South Wales with Norfolk Island, Victoria, South Australia, Queensland, and Western Australia; of Tasmania; of New Zealand; of Fiji; and of part of New Guinea.

In Australasia.

The stream of colonisation from modern Europe has flowed mainly due east or due west, and the southern current is of very recent date. It is really south-eastern rather than southern, an extension or diversion of European

CHAPTER VII.

enterprise and exploration in the East. Yet in quality and characteristics the Australasian colonies are more akin to the western than to the eastern provinces of the English Empire. They are settlements, not dependencies. In Australia the native element has never been strong, and is now, except in the northern districts, fast becoming extinct. In Tasmania the aborigines have wholly died out. In New Zealand the Maori race, with its fine physique and qualities, has decayed in the face of aggressive English immigration. In the Pacific islands alone the English are a ruling minority among a large native population. And not only are the British possessions in the Southern Seas colonies proper, in the sense of being comparatively empty lands populated and to be populated from the outside, but they have also from the first been peculiarly British to the exclusion of all other nationalities. Although the earliest explorers of Australia were not Englishmen[1], and the continent was first known to Europe as New Holland; although the alternative names of Tasmania and Van Diemen's Land alike recall the fact of Dutch discovery, while New Zealand takes its title from the famous province of the United Netherlands; yet the colonisation of Australasia has been left to Great Britain, undisturbed by any European rival; and it is only quite lately that the presence of the French and the Germans in some of the Pacific Islands has caused an apprehension in the minds of the Australian colonists, not that they will be interfered with within their present limits, but that they may not hereafter be able to claim the whole of the Australasian waters for their own. The geography of these southern colonies has fitted them to be the property of a maritime race, for they are a series of islands, beginning with the gigantic island of Australia. The whole of Australia is in English hands, and can be watched over by English fleets; and from the nature of the country,

---

[1] See Birdwood, p. 73, and references given in the last chapter. Torres Strait is called after a Spanish captain of that name.

apart from other reasons, the settlements have been kept mainly within measurable distance of the sea, girdling a vast extent of at present uninhabited interior.

To the fact of their insular position must be added also their temperate climate, which has placed them in the list of new homes for the English race. It is true that Fiji, New Guinea, and the protected Pacific Islands, are within the tropics; and that the extreme heat of the north of Australia, which is also in tropical latitudes, renders it unsuitable for European settlement. But the larger and far more important part of the Australian continent, with the adjoining island of Tasmania, lies within the temperate zone; and New Zealand has a climate still nearer akin than that of Australia to the climate of the British Isles.

In short, the English have been perhaps more fortunate in Australasia than in any other part of the globe. They have here found a vast extent open for settlement, with a climate and geographical position well suited for the work : and though England had no right of prior discovery, and attempted no colonisation in this quarter of the world till very recent years, she has been left to go her way unchecked by foreign interference or, except in New Zealand, by native wars, and has been allowed to develope this most valuable part of her empire in comparative quiet and peace.

22. The net result of English colonisation as a whole is that the United Kingdom, having an area of 120,832 square miles, and a population computed in the census of 1881 at 35,241,482, possesses a colonial empire, the area of which amounts roughly to 8,310,000 square miles, and the population to 216,000,000. Further the quality of this empire is as striking as the quantity, for it is estimated that three fourths of the British colonies are situated within the temperate zone[1].

General summary.

[1] Taken from Sir R. Rawson's Inaugural Address to the Statistical Society, Nov. 1884.

CHAPTER VII.

Europe finds us military outposts: the East, large dependencies with an overflowing native population: the West and the South, settlements in which the British breed may reproduce itself *ad infinitum*: and if the United States be included in the calculation of English colonies, as surely they ought to be, the sum total constitutes a record of colonisation absolutely without parallel in the history of the world.

England has gained by her losses.

23. There is one striking fact in the foreign and colonial history of England which should never be left out of sight. England has distinctly gained by her losses. Twice in her history she made a great effort and signally failed.

In the Middle Ages she tried to become mistress of France, but the battles of Crecy and Agincourt were fought and won in vain, and the Channel Islands have long been the only remnant of her Norman or French dominions. If she had succeeded in her attempt to become a continental power, she would have lost the advantage of her insular position; and would in all probability have been even less successful than other European nations in the sphere of colonisation, inasmuch as her front would have been more divided than that of purely continental countries, and she would have spent her energies in vainly trying to go two ways at once.

In the eighteenth century she mismanaged her North American colonies; and when they turned restive, she tried to coerce them and was utterly beaten.

If the proper aim of a nation is simply to own so many square miles of the earth's surface, there is no redeeming side to this failure. But if a people should look rather to leavening the world, and to building up strong and wholesome communities, then the loss of the United States was in a sense a gain. As far as can be judged, they have prospered in independence, at least as much as would have been the case if they had retained their allegiance to the English crown; and as years have gone on, they have

ENGLISH COLONISATION.

shown some inclination to draw closer again to the mother country.

CHAPTER VII.

Their loss set England free to work in other directions. She looked out for a new field for colonisation, and found it in Australia. So the net outcome of the War of Independence has been that the British race has not lost America, and has gained other parts of the world.

But a still greater result has followed from this defeat. England learnt thereby the true mode of dealing with colonies. Her liberal colonial policy in the present century, which stands out in brilliant contrast to the systems of other times and other nations, is the direct fruit of her greatest mistake and her most striking failure.

CHAPTER VIII.

CHANGES IN THE ENGLISH COLONIES DURING THE NINETEENTH CENTURY.

Chapter VIII.

Special character of nineteenth century.

1. Though the nineteenth century has brought great additions to the English Empire, it has been still more notable for the changes which have taken place during its years in the internal condition of the colonies, and in their relations to the mother country and to each other. Railways, steamers, and telegraphs, have been introduced; great social reforms have been carried; self-government has been granted to the larger colonies; and the confederation movement is still at work in its double form, colonial confederation on the one hand, imperial confederation on the other.

Some notice of these changes is necessary in any account of the English colonies, if only for the reason that they are entirely new features in the history of the world. There is nothing answering to them in the past; no parallel which can be made a guide in estimating their future effects. Other centuries have differed from each other more in degree than in kind, and can accordingly be justly compared one with another; but the great movements of the nineteenth century stand by themselves, as in the main absolutely different from anything else which has been seen in the world.

Scientific inventions.

2. Science has been the main factor in transforming the face of the globe, as it has been of late years transformed. Great inventors and engineers have worked a far mightier

CHANGES IN THE ENGLISH COLONIES. 119

revolution in history than all the statesmen and soldiers who have been leaders of their race. And as England has been beyond other countries the home of scientific inventions, so it is in her wide-spreading empire, and in the vast territory of the kindred American republic, that the fruits of such inventions have as yet been most conspicuous.

CHAPTER VIII.

It must be remembered too that but a few years have passed since the wonderful works, which have become part of every-day life, were first designed. The earliest railway on which the locomotive was used, the line between Stockton and Darlington, was only opened in 1825. The first steamer from England to the United States ran in 1838, and from England to Australia in 1852. Cooke and Wheatstone took out their patent for an electric telegraph in 1837. A submarine telegraph between Dover and Calais was not laid till 1850, and a similar line between Great Britain and America was not successfully laid till 1866. The Suez Canal was only opened for traffic in 1869, though to the present generation of travellers the time when it was not in existence seems to lie far back in the dark ages. The invention of the telephone is at present quite in its infancy. If, therefore, such enormous strides have been made in so short a space of time, it is difficult for an unscientific mind to place any bounds to the extent to which the world may be changed in the coming time by the application and development of the forces of nature.

3. A few illustrations will show the great effect which these inventions have already had on the English colonies. Take first the construction of ship-canals. It is true that they hardly come under the head of new scientific discoveries, for similar works were carried out in very early times by the Babylonians and Egyptians; and Xerxes facilitated his invasion of Greece by cutting a ship-canal through the isthmus of Mount Athos. But, at the same time, it may be safely said, that since the days of ancient

Effect of scientific inventions on the English colonial empire. Ship canals.

potentates, who held human life of no account, no work of such magnitude as the Suez Canal would have been attempted, in the absence of modern engineering appliances and of the aid of steam.

The Suez Canal.

The Suez Canal has opened a new road to the East shorter than that round the Cape. It has thereby brought India and the Eastern Colonies into closer communication with England. It has further increased the importance of our Mediterranean stations, has led to the occupation of Cyprus, and has made it difficult, if not impossible, to avoid all interference in Egypt. Being also an alternative and a shorter route to Australia, it has given the Australians, on their side, an interest in keeping open the communication, and has brought them, in short, more within the sphere of European politics than they were before. These are some of the results of an engineering work which is not yet twenty years old.

The Panama Canal.

In America a similar canal is now being cut through the isthmus of Panama; and though, as far as can be seen, the work will not be of such vast importance to the English empire as the Suez Canal, it is obvious that at least the whole group of West Indian colonies will be affected by it, and that a direct western line to Australia will be opened.

The cutting of these two isthmuses, one in the East and one in the West, concerns the whole world. But even canals, which improve communication in a single colony only, have a great and lasting effect in holding the different districts together. Such, for instance, is the result of the canals by which the falls and rapids impeding the navigation of the St. Lawrence are surmounted: they rectify the flaws in the waterway between Upper and Lower Canada, they ensure steady unbroken communication between the sea and the interior, and thus help in no small degree to weld together the provinces of the Dominion.

The Canadian Canals.

4. If the Suez Canal had been opened prior to the introduction of steam, its effect would have been then as now actually to shorten the distance between Europe and the East; and in proportion as the voyage was made shorter, communication between these two quarters of the world would have become quicker and more regular.

Steam and telegraphic communication.

The same two results, greater speed and greater regularity in communication, have been produced by the use of railways and steamers, though in a different way. Steam does not shorten the actual distance between two points, but it enables the same distance to be compassed in a shorter time. It makes communication more constant, not because there is less space within which obstacles may arise, but because the forces which are sufficiently powerful to stop a coach or a sailing-ship, will not stop a train or a steamer; and when electricity is brought into play, a point is reached at which, to use the common phrase, space and time are practically annihilated.

Certainly the speed of communication may be said to be increased, when telegrams are received at the Colonial Office before they are sent out from an Eastern colony; and the regularity of steamers, as compared with sailing vessels dependent on wind and tide, is illustrated by the accuracy of the Postal Services, and the readiness with which a great company enters into a contract with the government binding itself under forfeit to carry mails to certain places by certain definite dates. The time-table of the Peninsular and Oriental Company, for instance, shows that the company have contracted to carry mails from Brindisi every week to Bombay, and every fortnight to Madras and Calcutta, to China and to Australia[1]; and that the dates of arrival at and departure from the intermediate ports are fixed to the day, sometimes even to the hour. Communication

---

[1] The contract with the Imperial Government does not extend to the Australian service.

CHAPTER VIII.

Effects of the introduction of steam and electricity upon the mutual relations of the mother country and the colonies.

by sea has, in short, become almost as regular as communication by land.

5. From the trading point of view it is clear that the effects of the introduction of steam and electricity cannot be over-estimated. They tend to make the whole world one market—a natural consequence thwarted only by the artificial restrictions which the jealousies of different nations impose on each other's commerce. But apart from trade, it is interesting to notice the direct results of these forces upon the political and social relations of the component parts of the English empire.

During the present century the mother country has by these means been brought into infinitely closer and more systematic communication with the colonies, the colonies with the mother country and each other, and the various districts of each great dependency one with another.

There is now no colony, however remote, which is not connected with the outer world by a regular line of steamers. Even the Falkland Islands are periodically visited by the ships of a Hamburg company on their way to and from the Pacific ports of South America. There are further very few colonies which do not enjoy the benefits of a submarine telegraph; Mauritius being perhaps the most notable exception.

The large colonies too have completed or are rapidly developing systems of railways and inland telegraphs throughout their territory. The Cape now has three lines of rail carried at least as far as the Orange River. The South Australian government in 1872 laid a telegraph straight through the heart of the continent, from Adelaide in the extreme south to Port Darwin in the extreme north. And the great work of the Canadian Pacific Railway has just been finished, which spans the whole Dominion from the Atlantic to the Pacific.

No better illustration can be given than this last-named

railway to show what an important factor steam is in modern politics. British Columbia only joined the Dominion under the express stipulation, embodied in the Order in Council of the 6th of May, 1871, that such a line should be undertaken and carried out. In other words, this one work was in great measure the key to the problem of making British North America a single state with a seaboard on both oceans.

England and her colonies, then, are now in daily correspondence by the telegraph. Every steamer takes out Englishmen to one or other of the colonies, and brings back colonists to England. There are no long breaks of communication. If one ship is wrecked, two or three others arrive safely within a few days. If a telegraph cable gives way, there is probably another line still working, and the faulty cable is speedily repaired. Thus the great difficulty, with which ancient states had to contend, that of keeping a hold on distant dependencies, is now in great measure surmounted; and steam and electricity go far to counteract the natural tendency of peoples, who live at the other end of the earth, to separate more and more from their original home.

It is interesting to speculate whether this latter tendency will in the long run prevail, or whether railways, steamers, and telegraphs, will prove a stronger counteracting force. For instance, the older men among the Australians are mainly English born: many of the colonists have gone out quite lately from this country: and England, to an Australian, is in great measure synonymous with home. But it would be foolish to disguise the fact that, as years go on, generations must spring up who in a sense know not Joseph; a race of men to whom England will be the land of their fathers but not of themselves; who will find in Australia alone an ever-widening sphere for their ambitions, and an ever-growing stimulus to their interests; and in whose minds

CHAPTER VIII.

the sentiment for what is past and for what is distant will be weakened by the ties and the realities of the present.

Meanwhile, however, steam and electricity will be at work in direct opposition to this centrifugal tendency, promoting unity of interest, multiplying intercourse between these two parts of the world, and strengthening the bonds of common race and common language. It would indeed be difficult to prophesy which force will prevail in the future.

The tropical dependencies of England have been already contrasted with her settlements; but one additional and important point of contrast may here be noticed in connexion with the subject of steamers and railways. Englishmen have made their homes in Canada, Australasia, or South Africa; and while the effect of steam is to produce a constant interchange of visits, the Canadian or Australian, for instance, goes back to his colony after a while; or if he stays permanently in Great Britain, his place is more than filled up by fresh English emigrants. But in India, as has been seen, Englishmen do not make a lasting resting-place; consequently, while steamers and railways take out far more tourists to the East than would have travelled in old days, they also bring back Englishmen from the East at far shorter intervals than of yore. Where a man would stay twenty years in India without coming back to Europe, he now stays five or six, probably sending his wife and children back even sooner: consequently the East is even less of a home to English people than ever it was. The Anglo-Indian is more English and less Indian than he used to be: while still in India he gets ten English letters and newspapers to one he could have got in old days, and his mind and heart are more than ever set on his own country. So modern inventions have had in this case two almost contradictory effects. Since steam and electricity have been brought into play, both tourists and stayers at home hear and see much more of India and the Indians than their fathers did; but, on the other hand, those whose calling lies in the East spend their lives there in a much less degree than was the case in the past.

The government of the empire too has been entirely revolutionised by science. Where there is governing to be done, it is done to a far greater extent from home, and in a far more methodical and systematic way than in old times; while at the same time public opinion, both at home and in the colonies, is brought to bear on all foreign and colonial questions to a degree which was once unknown. So far as abuses are prevented by all the world knowing at once any important step taken by officials, and so far as a uniform system of administration is produced by regular correspondence, science has worked an unmixed good: but, from one point of view, the change wrought by modern inventions gives cause for regret. Governors and administrators must nowadays perforce be less self-reliant, more afraid of responsibility, and less capable of strokes of genius, than were their predecessors, although in most respects they are probably vastly superior.

A man who lives at the end of the telegraph wire, and within reach of the House of Commons, cannot think and act for himself as much as one who is cut off from the home government and is practically his own master: and now that each colony and dependency is brought into close connexion with the mother country, it is difficult to suppose that the class of men will yet be found in office, who, great alike in their merits and in their failings, built up the English Empire.

Among great Englishmen who have lately died, after having spent their lives in military or political service abroad, Sir Bartle Frere and General Gordon were, in their respective spheres, specially conspicuous for strength of character. The former was one of the old school of Indian administrators, who were trained by necessity to rely on themselves alone;

CHAPTER VIII.

and it is worth remembering that when he went to South Africa, and there initiated a strong forward policy, no submarine telegraph had as yet been laid to the Cape. General Gordon's greatness throughout his life was coupled with absolute independence of action and freedom from official control; and he was never so great as at the last, when all telegraphic connexion between Khartoum and the outer world had been hopelessly cut off.

Improved communication has created a more wholesome but at the same time a more prosaic *régime*. The age of chivalry is past, and the adventurers, who in Gordon's view made England great, will be no longer known.

Social changes.

Abolition of slavery.

6. Of the great social movements of the present century, there are two which have specially concerned the colonies. They are the anti-slavery and the anti-transportation movements. It has been already pointed out in a former chapter, that the opposition to slavery in any shape, as being an evil thing, is of quite recent growth, unparalleled in former stages of the world's history; and also that the particular form of slavery, against which humanity revolted at the end of the last and the beginning of the present century, was peculiarly identified with modern colonisation. Slavery was confined to the tropical plantation colonies; and it was fortunately only the smaller colonies, the West Indian group and Mauritius, which felt the effects of its abolition. But if the mistakes of English politicians had not taken the United States from Great Britain, the struggle between the slavery and anti-slavery parties, which in America culminated in one of the most formidable civil wars which the world has ever seen, would have taken place within the limits of the English dominion; and, being centred in the greatest of English colonies, might have shaken the whole fabric of the empire. As it was, this revolution in the social system of the West Indies has left its effects down to the present day, and the progress of these colonies as a whole has been far slower and

less satisfactory than that of the settlements and dependencies, where there was no slave question to be solved.

Slavery was abolished in 1834 by an act of the Imperial Parliament, which voted twenty millions sterling by way of compensation to the slave-owners. In other words, the home government at once altered by a single law the whole form of society in one part of the British dominions, and taxed the mother country to put down a moral wrong in the colonies. In doing so it possibly laid down no new principles; but at any rate it carried out two old principles to a further point than had yet been reached.

The absolute supremacy of the mother country to the colonies was a doctrine of long standing; but at a time, when the current of public feeling was setting against it, this doctrine was applied in its most drastic form, not merely to effect some political change, but to carry out a social revolution.

The other principle, that the parent nation should make some sacrifice for her children, was also well known if but seldom acted upon: but it had not been previously carried to the point of voting in lump a large sum of public money, in order to improve not the material but the moral welfare of the colonies, and in order to abolish in them a state of things which was offensive to public morality at home.

But the effect of the anti-slavery movement did not end with the emancipation of the West Indian slaves. This same current of feeling has had much to do with the retention and the extension of the English colonies in West Africa, unsatisfactory possessions as they are in most respects: and the party which favours a strong policy in Africa and elsewhere, and which does not shrink from the prospects of enlarging the bounds of the English Empire and increasing the numbers of its subjects, derives no small support from the class of men, who hold that England has a high calling

CHAPTER VIII.

to fulfil, and that, as she added to her debt to put down slavery, so she should be prepared to incur fresh obligations in order to introduce law and liberty into the darker regions of the globe.

The anti-transportation movement.

7. The opposition to the system of transportation was in great measure parallel to the anti-slavery movement. Archbishop Whately, and other high-minded men, attacked transportation, just as Wilberforce and his followers attacked slavery. Humanity to criminals is akin to humanity to slaves; but, as has been shown, transportation in the abstract cannot be considered to be, like slavery, essentially contrary to right and justice. Its immorality consists in the attendant circumstances and in the consequences which have been found by experience to flow from it: and it is chiefly, if not only, in England that a strong antipathy to the system has grown up.

As the slavery question in the main touched one group of colonies only, viz. the West Indies, so the transportation question affected one group only, viz. the Australian colonies. But while in the first case the mother country compelled the colonists to abandon a system which they liked, in the second the colonists, aided by supporters in England, compelled the mother country to abandon a system which she liked: and while the abolition of slavery was carried by a strong exercise of Imperial authority, the abolition of transportation was mainly due to a strong outburst of self-assertion on the part of the Australian colonists. Both movements were backed by the loudly expressed opinion of right-thinking men, and both were decided to a great extent on moral grounds. But the one was allied to the principle of Imperial supremacy, the other to the principle of colonial independence.

The colonies where slavery was abolished are Crown colonies, or near akin to Crown colonies; but the original home of transportation is now *par excellence* the land of self-governing communities. This connexion carries us on to notice the political changes which have marked the colonial history of the present century.

8. The colonial rules and regulations printed in the annual Colonial Office list divide the English colonies into three classes: "(1) Crown colonies in which the Crown has the entire control of legislation, while the administration is carried on by public officers under the control of the Home Government. (2) Colonies possessing Representative institutions but not Responsible government, in which the Crown has no more than a veto on legislation, but the Home Government retains the control of public officers. (3) Colonies possessing Representative institutions and Responsible government, in which the Crown has only a veto on legislation, and the Home Government has no control over any public officer except the Governor." Ceylon may be given as a sample of the first class, Barbados of the second, and Canada of the third. The Crown colony proper is under the benevolent despotism of the Colonial Office. The colony enjoying Responsible Government is practically independent, for the veto of the Crown on legislation is very rarely put into force. Between these two extremes are colonies in various stages of local autonomy; the tendency being to modify the strict Crown colony government by the gift of some kind of representative institutions as lately in the cases of Jamaica and Mauritius.

Chapter VIII.

Political changes. Three classes of English colonies.

9. Canada, the Cape, Newfoundland, and the great Australasian colonies (with the exception of Western Australia) are all in full possession of Responsible Government; and this voluntary conversion of subordinate into practically co-ordinate and independent communities has been a striking feature of the present century. It was a new thing in the history of the world for the mother country to pursue a definite policy of gradually making her colonies self-governing, as soon as they became able to stand by themselves. In ancient times colonies were either wholly separate from the parent

Grant of Responsible Government to the great colonies.

CHAPTER VIII.

state, or in a condition of absolute subjection to her. The Greek colonies, it has been seen, were independent communities from the first, whereas the various parts of the Roman empire had no vestige of independence beyond municipal rights. In modern history, the general tendency, till recent years, was rather to keep a tight hold on the colonies than to allow them to take their own course, and it was not until England had lost the United States, that she learnt the unwisdom of pushing too far the doctrine of the supremacy of the mother country. The lesson was not lost however on English statesmen, and for the last forty years the colonial policy of this country has proceeded on the lines of giving home rule in its widest sense to the North American, Australian, and South African colonies. Responsible government in the united provinces of Upper and Lower Canada dates from the year 1840: it was soon afterwards given to Nova Scotia, New Brunswick, and Prince Edward's Island: and in 1855 to Newfoundland. The same course was adopted at about the same date with regard to New Zealand and the Australian colonies, with the exception of Western Australia. In 1872 a similiar privilege was accorded to the Cape. The respective merits and demerits of this policy of converting the great colonies from subject into allied states cannot be discussed here. It has been shown that it was a wholly new departure; and it can hardly be questioned, first, that the distance between Great Britain and these growing communities necessitated some such step; secondly, that the only way to prevent the mother country from breaking down under the weight of her empire was to relieve the strain at the centre; and thirdly, that the policy has been broadly justified by its results: the consciousness of being able to separate, has taken away the wish, and the only complaint now heard, is not that the colonies want to leave the mother country, but that there are some politicians in the mother country who seem indifferent to the colonies.

CHANGES IN THE ENGLISH COLONIES.

10. But the grant of responsible government to various parts of the empire does not stand by itself. It was connected with the free-trade policy of England; and it brought with it the important measure of removing the Imperial troops from the self-governing colonies, and calling on the latter to provide in some measure for their own defence.

Chapter VIII. Connected with free-trade policy at home, and with the removal of Imperial troops from the colonies.

As regards the first of these two points, it is clear that the application of free-trade principles to the colonies, and the abolition of any differential duties in favour of their produce in the markets of Great Britain, or of British wares in the colonial markets, was in itself a long step towards recognising the colonies as independent units [1].

As to the second, it need hardly be said that if the colonies were given the privileges of self-government, it was but consistent to impose upon them the duties of self-defence. Consequently the Imperial troops in Australia and New Zealand have been replaced by local militias. In Canada English soldiers are to be found only at Halifax, which is regarded as an Imperial station. At the Cape the Imperial forces have been gradually reduced to a garrison at Cape Town. At the same time, it must be remembered that up to the present day all colonies alike have shared the protection of the Imperial fleet, to which they have contributed nothing; and it is quite a new suggestion that they might be ready to contribute in money or kind to the naval forces on which the whole empire relies.

11. The confederation movement is a later development of colonial policy than the measures taken to establish responsible government; yet confederation and independence are closely allied to each other, and in the first instance in which responsible government was given, viz. Canada, it was coupled with the union of the two Canadian Provinces.

Confederation—the great political work of the century.

Speaking broadly, the special political work of the nineteenth century has been to carry out confederation in one form or

---

[1] See Lord Grey, 'Letters on Colonial Policy,' vol. i. letter i.

GEOGRAPHY OF THE COLONIES.

CHAPTER VIII.

another, to find a compromise between small states and great empires, which will preserve the advantages of both, and to reconcile Local Autonomy with Imperial Unity. The central point of European politics has been the formation of the Federal German Empire, while in America the century has been marked by the successful struggle of Federalism in the United States, and by the equally successful working-out of the same principle in the Canadian Dominion.

Two forms of confederation in regard to the English empire.
(1) Colonial confederation.

12. In regard to the English colonies, the movement has been spoken of as having a double form, and Colonial Confederation has been mentioned as distinct from Imperial Confederation. By the former is meant the union of a group of colonies under one central government. By the latter, the scheme which has never yet taken substantial form, but which is at least as old as the time of Adam Smith[1], of admitting representatives of the colonies into the Imperial parliament, or at least into some kind of Imperial council. These two kinds of confederation are in a sense opposed to each other. The union of several small colonies into one large colony emphasises colonial independence; it is the very antipodes of the time-honoured doctrine 'divide et impera;' it implies strengthening each geographical division of the empire, and adding to the power of the various members to break off from the main body. Imperial confederation, on the other hand, is intended to be an equipoise to colonial independence, and to keep the colonies with the mother country by giving them a voice and an interest in matters of Imperial concern.

Passing over less important instances of colonial confederation in a subordinate form, such as that of the Leeward Islands, it is worth while to compare shortly Canada, where the principle has been actually put into practice, with Australia and South Africa, where it has been more than talked of.

[1] See 'Wealth of Nations,' chapter on Colonies, part iii.

To carry out successfully a measure of federal union, the parts to be united must not be so distant or so cut off from each other as to make a common centre a practical impossibility; differences of race, of religion, and interest must be harmonised; and there must be some present active reason for making such union seem desirable in the eyes of those who are immediately concerned. *Chapter VIII. Requisites for its success.*

In the Canadian Dominion the drawback of vast extent of territory is counterbalanced by the magnificent water communication, and by the fact that the habitable part of the land is in the main continuous; while, as has been noticed, the far-off Pacific province has been brought into touch with Ontario and Quebec by the trans-continental railway. Of the races which inhabit the Dominion, the Indians are so few in number that practically they can be left out of account; and great as have been the difficulties which have arisen from the distinction between English and French Canada, enough has been said of the assimilating qualities of the French, to show that they are by nature at least as likely as any other European people to settle down by the side of the English. *British North America.*

Lastly, the fact that the great United States line the whole southern frontier of Canada, has furnished a powerful motive for Canadian union, since the feeling of kinship between the two nations has unfortunately not yet killed out all mutual jealousies. There is no motive for combining so powerful as the fear of outward pressure, and the Canadians might not have confederated but for their sense of the necessity of presenting an undivided front to their powerful neighbours.

The confederation, then, of British North America, which began with the Dominion Act of 1867, and which would now be complete if Newfoundland could be induced to join her sister colonies, was destined to be successful, and has certainly hitherto fulfilled its destiny.

In Australia no measure of the kind has yet been carried out, although a considerable step has been taken towards it *Australia.*

CHAPTER VIII.

by the recent establishment of a Federal Council for the Australasian colonies; and although the idea of a Federal Congress for Australia was entertained as early as 1850, when the bill for giving constitutions to these colonies was before the Imperial parliament[1].

One great obstacle to confederation which existed in Canada, viz. division of race, does not exist in Australia, where the natives are an even more unimportant element of the population than they are in the Dominion, and all the colonists are practically one in race and language. But on the other hand, the geography of Australia makes for confederation of the separate parts in a far less degree than that of British North America.

The uninhabitable tracts of Australia are in the centre, cutting off North from South, and East from West; and there is no grand series of rivers and lakes to match the water system of Canada. Further, in the case of an island, the whole of which is under English rule, there can be no pressing fear of foreign interference, such as arises in Canada from the immediate neighbourhood of the United States. At the same time it is interesting to notice that the strongest impulse to Australian union, and the only one which seems capable of overpowering the mutual jealousies of the separate colonies, has been given by the remote prospect of complications with the Germans in New Guinea, and the French in New Caledonia and other Pacific islands.

South Africa.

In South Africa, the problem of confederation is more difficult than in either of the other two cases. The country is wanting in natural means of communication, and the differences of race and interest are more marked than in either America or Australia. There is a large native population to be taken into account. There is another European race beside the English in the field; and that

[1] See Lord Grey, 'Colonial Policy,' vol. ii. letter ix.

race is not one which has the French capacity for assimilation, for the Dutch Boers of South Africa are almost a proverb for isolation and rugged independence of character. Nor is it a question here of merely uniting communities which are already under one Imperial government; but any South African Confederation, to be successful, must include, with two very dissimilar English Colonies, two Dutch Republics and certain Native Territories. Lastly, in the present divided condition of the native tribes, there seems to be no pressing motive for union among the Europeans. When the Zulu power was strong, little objection was taken to the English annexation of the Transvaal; but when this strong native force had been broken and dispersed, and the fear of Zulu invasion had been dispelled, the desire of independence was reawakened in the Boers, they rebelled and re-established their republic. It is difficult to see at the present time from what source a bona fide movement towards confederation will arise. It can only be supposed and hoped that, as railways spread and bring the various districts with their diverse inhabitants into contact with each other, as commercial unity is seen to be desirable, and the restlessness of half-civilised provinces gradually gives place to settled peace, South Africa, which could not be prematurely hammered together, will half unconsciously become a single state.

It has been seen that pressure from without gives a strong impulse to confederation within. This applies to the British empire as a whole as well as to its component parts. A new life has been given to the doctrine of Imperial federation by the foreign troubles in which Great Britain has been of late years involved.

During the Sudan campaign, and when war with Russia was threatened, the Australian colonies took a very practical and very generous way of identifying themselves with the empire, by sending contingents of troops at their own cost to

(2) *Imperial confederation.*

the assistance of the mother country. By taking this step, they made it difficult in principle to resist the conclusion, that those who help to bear the cost should have a voice in the policy through which the cost is incurred.

Imperial Federation however is still little more than a dream of the future; which can, one would say, only become a waking reality, if steam, or electricity, or some yet undiscovered force, works fresh wonders in bringing the opposite poles of the earth together. Its advocates have as yet failed to show, either that the defects of the present system are so serious as to call for a vast and sweeping change in the relations between the mother country and the colonies, or that their ideal scheme offers advantages over the present order of things well worth any price that may be paid.

The one practical defect in the present system appears to be that the voice of the colonists is not sufficiently heard on the subject of the foreign policy of the empire. But this defect is already being gradually and unostentatiously remedied by the presence in this country of the Agents General for the great colonies, who are more and more recognised and consulted as the representatives of their respective communities on matters in which those communities are interested. On the other hand, the advantages to be gained by federation seem somewhat hypothetical. It is difficult to suppose that the interests of New Zealand would be furthered by the presence of New Zealand representatives in a distant federal assembly in which they would be insignificant units. And if it be argued that such federation would bring about greater unity of the different parts of the empire, it may be said with at least equal truth, that any scheme of the kind would only tend to emphasise and bring into prominence the great diversity of interests which exists within the bounds of the British Empire, and that the attempt to frame an artificial union would involve a risk of breaking up a system, which is based solely on mutual goodwill, unwritten and undefined, and on the consciousness of strength and independence which animates the great English colonies.

Again, as it would seem, the contention of the supporters of Imperial Federation implies that the English Empire should be exclusive as against the rest of the world. The noblest hopes for the future of the globe are directed to breaking down as far as possible the barriers between nations and races, whereas an English confederation, even if it included, as it is to be hoped it would include, the United States, would probably intensify the opposition between the Anglo-Saxon and other races. Politically it would make for Imperialism, commercially it would make for Protection.

The conclusion of the whole matter seems to be this: English colonisation has succeeded, because state interference has been at a discount and English citizens at home and abroad have worked out their own salvation. If this and other plain lessons of the past be taken for guidance in the coming time, the fate of the English Empire will be left to natural evolution, political theories will be looked at with suspicion, and short cuts even to Imperial Unity will be viewed with a well-based distrust.

INDEX OF PRINCIPAL NAMES.

Acadia. *See* Nova Scotia.
Aden, 69, 105, 109, 110, 111.
African dependencies of England, 110, 111, 112.
Albuquerque, 57, 68, 73.
American dependencies of England, 112, 113.
Angola, 68, 71.
Anguilla, 96, 112.
Antigua, 96, 112.
Asiatic dependencies of England, 109, 110.
Assiento compact, 37.
Athenian colonies, 8, 54, 55.
Athenians, 21, 55.
Australasian dependencies of England, 113, 114, 115.
Australia, 2, 8, 17, 18, 19, 23, 30, 35, 36, 43, 69, 75, 103, 106, 113, 114, 115, 123, 128, 129, 130, 131, 133, 134, 135.

Bacon, 1, 3 *n*., 40.
Bahamas, 96, 112.
Baltimore, Lord, 30, 95.
Barbados, 38, 95, 112, 129.
Basques, 10.
Basutoland, 107.
Batavia, 75.
Bencoolen, 102 *n*., 105.
Bermudas, 43, 95, 112.
Betshuanaland, 107.
Boers, 24, 135.
Bombay, 97.
Borneo, 69, 81, 105, 108, 109.
Bougainville, 103.
Bourbon. *See* Réunion.
Brazil, 31, 36, 39, 40, 41, 42, 60, 62, 69, 72, 76, 82, 87.
Bristol, 44, 64, 95.
British Columbia, 106, 123.
British Guiana, 101, 112, 113.
British Honduras, 102, 112.

British North Borneo company, 109.
Brooke, Rajah, 105, 108.
Burmah, 69, 75, 107.

Cabot, 60, 64, 93.
Cadiz, 49, 65.
Calcutta, 97.
California, 18, 62.
Canada, 2, 7, 10, 16, 19, 22, 25, 29, 36, 84, 87, 88, 100, 106, 112, 120, 122, 129, 132, 133, 134.
Canaries, 61.
Cape, 43, 68, 75, 79, 81, 91, 101, 111, 122, 129, 130, 131.
Cape Coast Castle, 96.
Cape de Verdes, 68.
Carthaginian colonies, 8, 36, 49-52, 54.
Carthaginians, 22, 47, 49-52, 80.
Cartier, 42, 82.
Cayenne, 40, 82, 89.
Ceylon, 12, 35, 69, 75, 77, 79, 81, 101, 102, 109, 110, 129.
Champlain, 10, 25, 82, 84.
China, 45, 69, 75, 105.
Chinese, 18, 19, 20, 24, 31, 45.
Clive, 57, 83.
Cochin China, 69, 75, 89.
Colbert, 82, 83, 85, 86.
Columbus, 4, 5, 10, 42, 60, 61, 63, 64.
Cook, 103.
Cortes, 25, 63.
Cromwell, 42, 96.
Cuba, 39, 40, 61.
Curaçao, 76.
Cyprus, 29, 49, 53, 104, 106, 109, 111.
Cyrene, 49, 52, 53.

Danes, 39, 90.
Darwin, 41.
Davis, 93, 105 *n*.

INDEX OF PRINCIPAL NAMES.

De Frontenac, 95.
Diaz, Bartholomew, 68.
Diego Garcia, 110.
Dominica, 100, 112.
Drake, Sir F., 5, 64, 93.
Dupleix, 25, 84, 87.
Dutch, 12, 21-26, 30, 39, 47, 51, 52, 74-81, 96, 107, 114, 135.
Dutch colonies, 74-81.
Dutch East India Company, 22, 30, 75, 77, 78, 94.

Egypt, 40, 111, 120.
Elmina, 68, 76.
English as colonisers, 7, 8, 12, 16, 19, 20, 22, 23, 26, 27, 30, 32, 33, 39, 42, 45, 47, 63, 90-117, 137.
English East India Company, 8, 22, 30, 78, 94, 96, 97, 98, 108.
European dependencies of England 109.

Falkland Islands, 105, 112, 113, 122.
Fiji, 104, 106, 113, 115.
Formosa, 69, 75.
Fort St. David, 97.
French, 7, 13, 16, 25, 37, 39, 40, 42, 44, 47, 81-89, 111, 112, 114, 133, 134.
French colonies, 81-89, 111, 112.
French East India Company, 78, 83, 86, 94.
Frere, Sir B., 125, 126.
Frobisher, 7, 42, 93.

Gambia, 68, 96, 110.
Gambia Company, 98.
Genoa, 60.
Georgia, 42.
Germans, 10, 16, 23, 114, 134.
Gibraltar, 43, 100, 109, 111.
Gilbert, Sir Humphrey, 93, 95.
Goa, 13, 68, 69, 72.
Gordon, General, 125, 126.
Greeks, 4, 5, 21, 22, 24, 26, 47, 48, 49, 51, 52-55, 56.
Greek colonies, 9, 14, 28, 52-55.
Grenada, 100, 112.
Griqualand West, 107.
Guano Islands, 45.
Guaranis, 13.

Guiana, 62, 76, 79.

Hakluyt, 93.
Halifax, 131.
Hawkins, 93.
Hayti. *See* St. Domingo.
Heeren, 34, 39.
Heligoland, 102, 109.
Henry Prince of Portugal, 10, 67, 71.
Hispaniola. *See* St. Domingo.
Hongkong, 36, 104, 105, 109, 110.
Hudson, 75.
Hudson Bay Company, 98, 106.
Huguenots, 13, 79, 82, 87.
Humboldt, 64, 65.

Iberians, 20, 49.
India, 3, 13, 16, 17, 25, 35, 45, 68, 69, 75, 83, 96, 97, 101, 102, 107, 108, 109, 110, 120, 124.
Indians, American, 25, 26, 31, 63, 65, 133.
Indies, Council of the, 66.
Irish, 10, 23.
Italians, 16.

Jamaica, 96, 98, 112, 129.
Jamestown, 97.
Java, 69, 75, 81.
Jesuits, 12, 13, 65, 87.
Jews, 24, 42.

Keeling Islands, 110.
Kimberley, Diamond fields of, 107.

Labourdonnais, 87, 101.
Labuan, 105, 108, 109, 110.
Lagos, 106, 110.
Leeward Islands, 100, 112, 132.
Lewis, Sir G., 1 *n.* 2, 2, 52.
Lisbon, 73.
Livingstone, 10.

Madagascar, 68, 83, 89.
Madeira, 49, 68.
Madras, 97.
Magellan, 62.
Malacca, 69, 75, 105, 109.
Malay peninsula, 102, 105, 110.
Maldives, 69, 109.
Malta, 49, 101, 109, 111.
Manilla, 62.

INDEX OF PRINCIPAL NAMES.

Manitoba, 106.
Maoris, 2, 32, 114.
Mariannes or Ladrones Islands, 62.
Maryland, 30, 95 *n.*
Mascarenhas, 68.
Massachusetts, 98.
Mauritius, 45, 69, 75, 89, 101, 110, 122, 126, 129.
Melbourne, 18.
Mestizoes, 34 *n.*
Mexico, 62.
Moluccas, 69, 81.
Montcalm, 84, 101.
Moravians, 12.
Mozambique, 68.

Nantes, Revocation of edict of, 13, 87.
Natal, 107, 110, 111.
Nevis, 96, 112.
New Brunswick, 95, 130.
New Caledonia, 44, 89, 134.
Newfoundland, 89, 94, 95, 112, 129, 130, 133.
New Guinea, 8, 69, 81, 109, 113, 115, 134.
New South Wales, 2, 34, 43, 103, 106, 113.
New York, 76, 98.
New Zealand, 2, 32, 75, 106, 113, 114, 115, 130, 131, 136.
Norfolk Island, 103, 113.
North America, 7, 16, 22, 23, 35, 38, 42, 63, 77, 98, 100, 112, 113.
Northmen, 5.
North West Territories, 106.
Norwegians, 16.
Nova Scotia, 82, 87, 95, 130.

Oglethorpe, 42.

Pacific Islanders, 45.
Panama Canal, 120.
Paraguay, Missions of, 13, 65.
Paris, Peace of, 100, 102, 103.
Paulistas, 41.
Penang, 102, 109.
Penn, 30.
Pennsylvania, 30.
Pericles, 55.
Perim, 105, 109, 111.
Peru, 35 *n.*, 45, 62.
Philippines, 60, 61, 62.

Phoenician colonies, 48, 49.
Phoenicians, 5, 20, 21, 22, 24, 47, 48, 49, 50, 53, 69.
Pitcairn Island, 28, 29.
Pizarro, 63.
Plassey, 101.
Plymouth Company, 98.
Pondicherry, 83, 89.
Porto Rico, 61.
Portuguese, 12, 16, 21, 22, 27, 30, 39, 42, 47, 60, 67-74, 77, 78, 79.
Portuguese Brazil Companies, 72.
Portuguese colonies, 67-74, 111.
Prince Edward Island, 106, 130.
Puritans, 4, 14, 28, 39, 97.

Quakers, 13, 39.
Quebec, 82, 100.
Queensland, 34, 106, 113.

Raleigh, Sir W., 5. 93.
Réunion, 68, 83, 89.
Richelieu, 82, 87.
Rodriguez, 69, 110.
Roman colonies, 8, 57-59.
Romans, 21, 26, 27, 47, 48, 55-59, 90.
Royal African Company, 96, 98.
Russians, 59, 90.

St. Domingo, 38, 42, 61, 85, 95.
St. Helena, 68, 75, 96.
St. Kitts, 96, 112.
St. Lucia, 101, 112.
St. Vincent, 100, 112.
Sarawak, 108.
Seville, 65.
Seychelles, 110.
Sicily, 49, 50, 51, 53, 56.
Sierra Leone, 43, 103, 110.
Singapore, 105, 109, 110.
Smith, Adam, 31, 54, 70, 132.
Socotra, 69.
South Africa, 19, 23, 26, 33, 36, 107, 111, 126, 134, 135.
South America, 16, 22, 23, 26, 34, 38, 62, 113.
Spaniards, 6, 11, 12, 16, 20, 22, 23, 25, 26, 27, 30, 31, 32, 39, 47, 49, 60, 61-67.
Spanish colonies, 14, 61-67.
Spice Islands, 62, 81.

Straits Settlements, 102, 109.
Suez canal, 119, 120.
Sulu archipelago, 62.
Surat, 83.
Surinam, 76.
Swedes, 16, 90.
Sydney, 18.

Tasmania, 41, 75, 103, 113, 114, 115.
Tobago, 100, 112.
Transvaal, 107, 135.
Trinidad, 102, 112.
Tristan d'Acunha, 68.
Turks, 27.
Turks Islands, 96, 112.

United States, 3, 10, 14, 15, 16, 19, 22, 23, 36, 38, 39, 43, 75, 97, 98, 100, 116, 119, 126, 132, 133, 134.

Utrecht, Peace of, 95.

Vasco de Gama, 61, 67, 68.
Venice, 51, 60.
Victoria, 34, 36, 44, 106, 113.
Virgin Islands, 96, 112.
Virginia and Virginia Company, 8, 9, 30, 44, 97, 98.

Wandewash, 101.
West Africa, 2, 16, 17, 39, 68, 75, 82, 89, 96, 103, 106, 110, 127.
Western Australia, 43, 106, 113, 129.
West Indies, 12, 31, 35, 38, 40, 42, 45, 62, 76, 82, 89, 95, 96, 99, 101, 113, 120, 126.
Wolfe, 83, 100.

Xavier, Francis di, 13.

THE END.

www.ingramcontent.com/pod-product-compliance
Lightning Source LLC
Chambersburg PA
CBHW022117160426
43197CB00009B/1067